OWNING MEMORY

Recent Titles in
Contributions in Librarianship and Information Science

The Impact of Emerging Technologies on Reference Service and
Bibliographic Instruction
Gary M. Pitkin, editor

Brief Tests of Collection Strength: A Methodology for All Types of
Libraries
Howard D. White

Censorship and the American Library: The American Library Association's
Response to Threats to Intellectual Freedom, 1939–1969
Louise S. Robbins

Librarianship and Legitimacy: The Ideology of the Public Library Inquiry
Douglas Raber

Scholarly Book Reviewing in the Social Sciences and Humanities: The Flow
of Ideas Within and Among Disciplines
Ylva Lindholm-Romantschuk

Libraries, Immigrants, and the American Experience
Plummer Alston Jones Jr.

Preparing the Information Professional: An Agenda for the Future
Sajjad ur Rehman

The Role and Impact of the Internet on Library and Information Services
Lewis-Guodo Liu, editor

Development of Digital Libraries: An American Perspective
Deanna B. Marcum, editor

Diversity in Libraries: Academic Residency Programs
Raquel V. Cogell and Cindy A. Gruwell, editors

Immigrant Politics and the Public Library
Susan Luévano-Molina, editor

Vandals in the Stacks? A Response to Nicholson Baker's Assault on
Libraries
Richard J. Cox

OWNING MEMORY

How a Caribbean Community Lost Its Archives and Found Its History

JEANNETTE ALLIS BASTIAN

Contributions in Librarianship and Information Science, Number 99
Richard J. Cox, Series Adviser

A Member of the Greenwood Publishing Group

Westport, Connecticut • London

Library of Congress Cataloging-in-Publication Data

Bastian, Jeannette Allis.
    Owning memory: how a Caribbean community lost its archives and found its history /
Jeannette Allis Bastian.
        p.   cm.—(Contributions in librarianship and information science; no 99)
    Includes bibliographical references (p.)
    ISBN 0–313–32008–X (pbk. : alk. paper)
    1. Archives—Virgin Islands of the United States.   2. Virgin Islands of the United
States—Historiography.   3. Memory—Social aspects—Virgin Islands of the United
States.   I. Title.   II. Series.
CD3985.V5B37   2003
027.07297'22—dc21   2003054609

British Library Cataloguing in Publication Data is available.

Library of Congress Catalog Card Number: 2003054609
ISBN: 0–313–32008–X
ISSN: 0084–9243

First published in 2003

Libraries Unlimited, 88 Post Road West, Westport, CT 06881
A Member of the Greenwood Publishing Group, Inc.
www.lu.com

Printed in the United States of America

The paper used in this book complies with the
Permanent Paper Standard issued by the National
Information Standards Organization (Z39.48–1984).

10   9   8   7   6   5   4   3   2   1

For Isabel, Madison, and Zeke.
A new generation.

CONTENTS

PREFACE

The construction of community memory is a hotly debated issue as historians, social scientists, literary critics, and others grapple with increasingly contested and reinterpreted pasts. Rarely heard is the voice of the archivist into whose care the documents of the past are entrusted, even though it is the archives that contain many of the key pieces to this puzzle. Without historical documents can communities build reliable and durable memory? It was this question plus the strong conviction that archivists needed to define a role for themselves in the memory debates that fueled my interest in pursuing this study of the community memory of a postcolonial society, the United States Virgin Islands. My concern was driven by the recognition that behind the theoretical discussions lies the practical reality that ownership of history (and therefore memory) is often obtained through hard-fought battles with uncertain outcomes for small disenfranchised societies or groups.

In the mid-1970s I relocated to the U.S. Virgin Islands where I began working as a librarian in the territorial library system. We regularly received requests for material that we did not own—the historical records of the Virgin Islands. The bulk of these records were in the Danish National Archives in Copenhagen or in the U.S. National Archives in Washington, D.C. The most that the library could provide, with the few microfilm copies of crucial records that had been purchased from these national institutions, was inadequate to answer all but superficial questions dealing with family history. We certainly could not satisfy the inquiries of researchers and historians pursuing the primary sources of Virgin Islands history. Fifteen years later, when I was the director of the Territorial Library and was attempting to establish an archive, I again confronted this hole in Virgin Islands history, this time as an archivist, knowing that all I had were fragmented documents, remnants of the past that could never be fashioned into a whole and seamless cloth.

This book tells the story of a small island community, the United States Virgin Islands—formerly a Danish colony, now a U.S. possession—that lost its historical memory when its archives were removed from the islands. Following the sale of the islands to the United States in 1917, the archives of the former Danish West Indies were transferred to national archives in both Denmark and the United States, making them virtually inaccessible to Virgin Islanders, descendents of the enslaved Africans brought to this plantation colony in the seventeenth and eighteenth centuries.

The dramatic effects of the loss of their archives on the efforts by Virgin Islanders to internalize and document their own cultural and colonial history provides a framework for examining the broader issues of memory in the relationship between communities and their historical records. These issues include both archival ones of records creation, provenance, access, and custody, as well as societal ones touching on the writing of history, the reconciliation of oral and written traditions, and the many ways that communities consolidate their memories. In addition, questions of archival power play crucial roles in colonial environments as the lack of access to historical records highlights and emphasizes their value in shaping memory.

Research and writing should not occur in isolation, and I appreciate the efforts of all who have assisted me in my quest. In particular I wish to thank Richard J. Cox, mentor extraordinaire, who, in addition to guiding me throughout the long process of developing and writing this book, also served as a reader for the final product. Particular thanks also to my two other voluntary readers, Donna Webber and Alan Perry, who were extremely generous with their time, perceptive in their comments, and unflagging in their encouragement. I also thank Svend Holsoe, who not only shared his vast knowledge of the Danish West Indian archives and Danish West Indian history but also provided intellectual balance and clarity to an emotion-laden subject.

This book is the fruit of living and working within a society that nurtured me, an outsider, over many wonderful years. I will be grateful always to my colleagues in the Virgin Islands library system—Marlene Hendricks, June A. V. Lindqvist, Robert Moron, Blanche Souffront, and Christian Doute, who taught me to appreciate the richness and unique nature of Virgin Islands culture. I would also like to thank all those who so generously discussed the issues of Virgin Islands history, memory, and community with me: Roy Adams, Aimery Caron, Lois Hassell Habteyes, Rosary E. Harper, Arnold Highfield, Derek Hodge, Svend Holsoe, Daniel Price Hopkins, Myron Jackson, Orville Kean, Marilyn Krigger, Lauren Larsen, Gregory LaMotta, Elizabeth Rezende, Robin Sabino, Malik Sekou, Gilbert Sprauve, Governor Charles Turnbull, and George Tyson.

I have been extremely fortunate in receiving more than my share of personal support and encouragement from my family. I would like to thank our children and their partners, Clay, Mag, Fiamma, David, Maureen, my brother Geoffrey, and most particularly my husband, Calvin F. Bastian, who has served as a constant touchstone for this book and whose insights, understanding, and love of the Virgin Islands continue to inspire me.

1

A COMMUNITY OF RECORDS

INTRODUCTION

On March 31, 1917, the Caribbean islands of the Danish West Indies were transferred with due ceremony from their colonizer, Denmark, to their purchaser, the United States, and were renamed the United States Virgin Islands.[1] Over the next four decades, the historical records of these islands dating back to their founding in the seventeenth century and including the detailed minutiae of all aspects of a 250-year-old colonial society were quietly transferred to the Danish National Archives and the National Archives of the United States. By the 1960s only property records and local police records remained in the islands. Even the early twentieth-century records of American rule had been gradually removed, and Virgin Islanders had to travel abroad to find their own history.

The effect of the loss of access to their archives on the ability of the Virgin Islands' people to write their own history and construct their collective memory forms the nucleus of this study. In a wider sense, this story of colonial records also concentrates our attention on the general relationships between archival records and the communities that create them, between records and memory and between memory and access. These relationships are examined through the lens of the United States Virgin Islands, a small community in the Caribbean Sea with a population of approximately 120,000 people divided among the three major islands of St. Thomas, St. Croix, and St. John. The majority of the current population are primarily descendents of the Africans brought to the islands as slaves in the eighteenth and early nineteenth centuries. Through the language of treaties, the interpretation of archival principles, climatic influences, and the conditions of colonialism, this former plantation colony lost access to its historical records. The consequences of this loss to the identity and memory of the community is investigated from the perspective of written histories of the islands, popular commemorations of historical events, and interviews with Virgin Islanders themselves.

How do Virgin Islanders forge their collective memory, and how does the absence of historical records impact on that process? Because the enslaved and free colored society in the Virgin Islands under Danish rule was primarily oral rather than written, the effect of that orality on the creation of records is also evaluated, in particular the tensions between the written word and the oral tradition. The value of the written record as collective memory is weighed within the context of both a colonial and an oral society. Finally, because this story is ultimately about archives, it also examines archival principles—particularly those that define ownership, custody, and access—in terms of how these principles assist or discourage the process of memory building.

The value of the Danish West Indian and the early American records to the U.S. Virgin Islands today not only lies in the historical facts surrounding their creation and content but is also bound up with the community's spiritual and emotional ties to the enslaved African society that lies at the heart of Virgin Islands identity. In the Danish West Indies, written records were created primarily by and for the colonizing Danish bureaucracy. The enslaved Africans and free colored peoples who made up the bulk of the Danish West Indian population were for the most part nonliterate. The official records were written in Danish even though the lingua franca of the non-Danish inhabitants of the islands were primarily English and Dutch Creole. However, the fact that these records were neither created by nor written for the majority of the population does not lessen their importance as a means for understanding the history of these islands and reconstructing the identity of its peoples. Rather, it suggests that, in order to use records as reliable indicators of an entire society, both the subjects as well as the creators of the records must be seen as active participators in a process in which record creating is defined as much by place, people, and community as it is by the act of creation itself.

The dynamic use of records to understand the lives and history of an entire community, including those who are not literate or who, for other reasons have no voice, is posited through a historical methodology developed by French historian Marc Bloch. Writing in the 1930s, Bloch suggested that the records of a society are "witnesses in spite of themselves."[2] That is, on the one hand, the records become witnesses in the evidentiary sense arising from the process of record making and record keeping itself and, on the other, also bear witness to the lives of those who are the subjects of the records. The records speak for those whose voices are otherwise silent. Through listening to these whispers in the records while understanding the record-making and -keeping process itself, we are able to hear all the voices involved in their creation.

From an archival standpoint, understanding the context and structure of the record brings a rich, expanded content into focus so that, for example, a census record or a slave auction notice not only highlights these actions themselves and the nature of the society in which they were taking place but also conveys information about the individual lives being acted on. The voiceless speak to us through these bureaucratic records and compel us to reconsider and define the record-keeping activities of a community in broad and inclusive terms. This Virgin Islands story of the relationship of records to communities and to their collective memory expands our understanding of archival provenance by describing a dynamic synergy between a community and its records, in which records enable access to a past that seems otherwise unreachable. In this context, provenance, the key organizational basis of archival arrangement and description, goes beyond the standard definitions that, first, refer to the maintenance of records by their creator or source and, second, stipulate that records from different creators must not be intermingled, to suggest that provenance may describe the context of an entire society, not only the creators of records but the subjects of them.

This is not a new concept in the archival literature. As the complexity of modern records creation has put an ever-increasing burden on the principle of provenance, provenance itself has expanded to embrace both the specific processes of records production and the wider society within which the records were created. As early as 1970, Canadian archivist Hugh Taylor noted that "archivists ought to focus more on why and how people have created documentation, rather than on their subject content. Archivists should extend their understanding of the provenance of documentation deeply in to the societal origins of human communication throughout history."[3] In the new century, provenance is linked to postmodernism by another Canadian archivist, Tom Nesmith, who further refines provenance to embrace "the societal and intellectual contexts shaping the action of the people and institutions who made and maintained the records, the functions the records perform, the capacities of information technologies to capture and preserve information at a given time, and the custodial history of the records."[4] Collective memory, which similarly coalesces around the contexts created by people, events, locales, processes, and societal movements, also becomes a factor in the provenance considerations that archivists confront. In this definition, the records of a community become the products of a multitiered process of creation that begins with the individual creator but can be fully realized only within the expanse of this creator's entire society. The records of individuals become part of an entire community of records.

A COMMUNITY OF RECORDS

The phrase "community of records" refers to the community both as a record-creating entity and as a memory frame that contextualizes the records it creates. Although tensions between oral and written traditions as well as ambiguity within the records themselves may temper and influence the interpretation of records produced in colonial societies, these societies nonetheless share the compelling need to document that characterizes those communities of records that we often associate with Western civilization but that in reality extend globally. The need to record in some format is a feature of all societies. Social anthropologist Jack Goody ties the development of writing directly with an economic need to keep records. He uses the quipu (knotted cords of the Inca) to illustrate that record keeping predates and foreshadows actual writing itself. Pointing out that "a complex state exercises pressures in favour of the development of a recording system especially if its central finances are based upon the collection of tax or tribute,"[5] Goody presents a powerful argument for a society's need for increasingly sophisticated methods of record keeping as the society itself becomes more complex. This view is supported by Henri-Jean Martin who writes that "a society creates a writing system when it has attained a certain level of development, when the concentration of its population reaches a new high and when it attempts to respond to a global acceleration (in the broadest sense of the term)."[6]

The development of writing for record keeping since the time of the ancient Sumerians is well documented,[7] emphasizing the purely functional use of records for administrative and commercial purposes. The need to keep an accounting of property and taxation between a government and its citizens, the necessity of inscribing transactions of goods and services between individuals and between nations, drove (and continues to drive) society's dependence on record keeping. The multiple layers of a society's interaction with its government and within itself generate its own complex network of records. Society's need for the extended memory and evidence provided by written records has compelled the existence of archives or, as Canadian archivist Terry Cook observes, "behind the record is the need to record."[8] Though it may seem that the proliferation of records is a phenomenon of modern society, this is due more to the multiple means that currently exist of creating and reproducing records than to the need for record keeping itself. The imperative to record is ancient, modern, and ubiquitous, crossing temporal, cultural, and geographic lines. It ranges from a government imposing control on its citizens through taxation or an individual making her voice heard through a diary or a vote, to a legal need for written proof of property lines or exchanges of goods and services, and from a desire to retain memories through scrapbooks, letters, and photographs to the democratic imperative to establish accountability between the state and its citizens. Societies at all levels of sophistication have a relationship with the act of recording in some form or format, be it the knots of the Incas, the totems of Native Americans, or the paintings of early cave dwellers.

It is through recording in fully literate communities, however, that record keeping is woven into the very fabric of society, underpinning the foundations of governments, defining the boundaries of societies, and framing individual lives. If the need to record is inseparable from the act of recording, then the record is the representative of that need, remaining as tangible evidence of an action taken, a sentiment expressed, a transaction conveyed, a position stated. Through this relationship between actions and records, communities are defined. The actions of communities, expressed in a wide variety of prescribed ways, both written and oral, create a mirror in which records and actions reflect one another in documenting the activities and forming the memory of the community. At the same time, a community of records is also one in which traditions of record keeping are developed, manifested, and bounded by recognized and accepted conventions in the drafting of particular types of documents. For example, Pauline Maier, in her study of the writing of the Declaration of Independence, notes that the rebellious American colonists followed traditional and prescribed forms of documentation that were well established in England to construct their declaration of freedom to the British king.[9] They followed these forms partly because they had carried that record-keeping tradition with them to the New World and partly because they understood that their petition would be considered seriously only if it were written in an acceptable and recognizable form. Forms and modes of expression, or record structures, are shared between record-creating communities, creating in turn "imagined communities" of records similar to those envisioned by Benedict Anderson in his classic work on nationalism.[10]

A community of records may be further imagined as the aggregate of records in all forms generated by multiple layers of actions and interactions between and among the people and institutions within a community. Layers of records parallel the active life of the community itself. At the bureaucratic level, these records may include tax and property records, drivers' licenses, birth certificates, or voter registration; at a personal level they include letters, scrapbooks, diaries, and checkbooks. In form of expression they could include folktales, parades, commemorations, and performances. These nonwritten records also generally fit within formats recognized and accepted by the entire community. The records of a community not only are the evidence of the actions and transactions of the individuals within the community but also define the public consciousness of the community itself. Records, oral or written, become both the creators as well as the products of the societal memory of a community.

The existence of inherent relationships between historical records and the communities that create them is implicit in the very existence of archival collections. Archivist Ernst Posner has suggested that "the keeping of archives . . . constitutes a significant aspect of mankind's experience in organized living" and that without archives, "the story of our past could not be told."[11] Scholars in other disciplines concur that the making of records to document aspects of living constitute an early use of writing.[12] At the same time, it is also clear from the history of humankind's involvement with writing that the use of records to document everyday life is only one of the reasons that communities make and keep records.

The development of bodies of records preserved and valued by communities over time suggests that the keeping of archives goes beyond the need to account for the past and speaks to other felt needs within the communities themselves, the primary one being that of community (or national) identity.[13] Many of the basic archival principles, such as custody and provenance, that ensure and safeguard the authenticity of records also give substance to the ability of records to support and foster collective memory and identity. Efforts to repatriate archival materials, whether through copying or by actual physical exchange, point to the self-affirming role of records as cultural heritage.

The collective memory of the community is framed within the wide definition of the records that it creates, a definition that embraces not only written documentation but also the many forms of remembrance and recording that include oral traditions, public ceremonies, commemorations, artifacts, and markers such as public statues and private grave sites. To construct and maintain reliable memory, however, communities above all require access to their written documents, ownership of the primary sources of their history. This access is provided at least in part by social institutions such as archives and museums, but, as the Virgin Islands case demonstrates, the access needs of all the record creators are not necessarily considered in assigning the custodianship and ownership of records.

RECORDS AND MEMORY

The relationship between communities, memory, and written records is complex and multifaceted. The reflective, reinforcing, and remembrancing roles that historical records play in the construction of community memory support the evidential, authenticating, and factual roles. Vital to all such roles must be ability of the community to access the records to build and defend that memory. Here the archival role becomes paramount. Through the accession, appraisal, preservation, housing, and maintenance of a community's written records, archivists facilitate the construction of memory. The critical importance of an archive as a both a physical and spiritual "house of memory" in which records are united and stored is underscored when considering the dilemmas faced by communities whose archives are lost, whether through war, conquest, or natural or man-made destruction. Of particular consideration are the difficulties faced by many postcolonial countries, whose fragmented and fragile records often exist thousands of miles apart.

Recognition of the profound emotional as well as historical value of records to the identity of a newly formed political entity provided the impetus for many former colonies, such as the United States and Canada, to engage in copying projects to retrieve and repatriate the valuable documentation related to their settlement and founding. In the United States, for example, copying projects were initiated in the early nineteenth century, fueled by a growing interest in historic materials and the wave of patriotic enthusiasm following the American Revolution. When state historical societies realized that their historic documents were incomplete, they requested and received financing from state legislatures for journeys to England and other European countries for the transcribing of relevant documents. The first such venture was undertaken by Georgia in 1824, quickly followed by other eastern and southern states.[14] The concern with accessibility to documentary heritage, for example, was the focus of an early-nineteenth-century New York state legislative act sending John Romeyn Broadhead on an extended three-and-a-half-year journey to Europe to copy documents in England, the Netherlands, and France. The act authorizing the trip clearly describes its intentions regarding both the need to have accessibility to the state's documentary heritage and its hope to somehow procure the original documents:

An agent shall be appointed by the Governor of this State, by and with the advice and consent of the Senate to visit England, Holland and France, for the purpose of procuring, if possible, the originals, and if not, copies, of all such documents and papers, in the archives and offices of those governments relating to or in any way affecting the Colonial or other history of this State, as he may deem important to illustrate that history.[15]

Following New York's success, other states followed suit, and documania became a national obsession with an unending stream of American scholars making the pilgrimage to British and European depositories during the mid-nineteenth century, bringing back records that were generally published before being deposited in state historical societies.[16] Collecting historical documents was the primary reason for the formation of the historical societies, and they often served as surrogate state archives.[17] The public's desire for an accessible documentary heritage was intense and "part of the incentive for the publishing of primary sources was, of course, to establish stronger state and national identities, basically the same reason why so many of the early state histories were being written and published in the early republic."[18]

At the same time, while the formation of a documentary heritage in the United States was being achieved at a state level, reclaiming history through the copying of key documents in Europe became a central mission of the Public Archives of Canada. The dilemma of joint heritage inherent in acquiring and preserving documents of a history entangled within the relationships of colonialism was immediately appreciated by the Public Archives. They recognized that, due to the nature of its history and its relationship with the colonizing country, Canada could not be studied without access to archival resources in Great Britain, France, and Ireland.[19] Rather than engage in disputes with European nations over transferring archives, custodial rights, or who would hold the original documents, both the Canadians and the Americans were fortunately able to finance the copying of their records and resolve the shared aspects of their heritage early on in their histories.

In the case of small, less affluent, postcolonial entities with harsh, contested, and terrible pasts, such as the U.S. Virgin Islands, this dilemma has been more difficult to resolve. To appreciate the Virgin Islands situation within the context of its plantation history, it is important to ask the following question: For the former colonies of the Caribbean, whose current populations have no history in the Caribbean before the arrival of enslaved Africans to its shores, how vital are colonial records to their need for collective memory and a sense of history?

In 1963, British/Trinidadian author V. S. Naipaul despairingly (and famously) described his perception of the dilemma of Caribbean history in his early seminal work, *The Middle Passage:*

How can the history of this West Indian futility be written? What tone shall the historian adopt? Shall he be as academic as Sir Alan Burns, protesting from time to time at some brutality, and setting West Indian brutality in the context of European brutality? Shall he, like Salvador de Madriaga, weigh one set of brutalities against another, and conclude that one has not been described in all its foulness and that this is unfair to Spain? Shall he, like the West Indian historians, who can only now begin to face their history, be icily detached and tell the story of the slave trade as if it were just another aspect of mercantilism? The history of the islands can never be satisfactorily told. Brutality is not the only difficulty. History is built around achievement and creation; and nothing was created in the West Indies.[20]

Fifty years earlier, Waldemar Westergaard, Danish/American author of the first history of the Danish West Indian islands had likewise observed that "treated by itself, colonial history is well-nigh meaningless. Only when considered as part of European history—indeed, when related somehow to universal history—does it become vital."[21]

Despairing acknowledgments of "historylessness," from very different perspectives, are expressed both by Caribbean poet and Nobel Prize laureate Derek Walcott and by Caribbean historian Michel-Rolph Trouillot, who share similar senses of archival loss as they contemplate the silences in the recorded histories of their own Caribbean countries.[22] Walcott wryly observes that "what is archival in the Caribbean, as the Caribbean writer knows, is what got lost in the annals of sugar cane burned every harvest like the library of Alexandria, what disappeared in spray in the wake of the slaves. A huge amnesia rather than a history."[23] Trouillot notes the silences in the creation of the sources (archives) themselves, the things left out, not deliberately but because at the time they seemed peripheral and not important to the central historical narrative that was taking place. He writes, "Silences are inherent in the creation of sources, the first moment of historical production. Unequal control over historical production obtains also in the second moment of historical production, the making of archives and documents." As an example of the silences in the creation of sources, Trouillot refers to plantation birth records in which slave births were not recorded until it was seen that the child survived. He points out that the "silence" did not occur through negligence, nor through the wish to conceal anything; rather, "both births and deaths were actively silenced in the records for a combination of practical reasons inherent in the reporting itself."[24] Both writers see not a memory loss but a historical hole where the history of a whole segment of the population never existed. Not a history forgotten, but one that was never recorded and therefore not remembered. Similarly, a researcher of Danish West Indian historical geography uses identical terminology to describe the historical gap created by Danish colonialism. In an interview he speaks of a historical hiatus that Virgin Islanders must confront, "a black hole in history in which they can glimpse little besides the horror and degradation of enslavement," which he describes as both a moral and a historiographical darkness.[25]

Within a few years of the publication of *The Middle Passage*, a study, *Decisions of Nationhood: Political and Social Development in the British Caribbean*, defined some of the ideological as well as practical issues that the aspiring nations of the Caribbean would have to confront if they were to become successfully independent. The authors, Wendell Bell and Ivar Oxaal, argue that determining the new nation's cultural tradition is one of the "big decisions of nationhood." They point out that "one of the major means of cultural management is to be found in the way a nation's version of its own social and cultural history is written and rewritten," and that "as in other nations, the people of the West Indies draw on their conceptions of their own history for some understanding of themselves, for what they and their nations mean and stand for." Although archives will help scholars analyze events, discredit some interpretations, or formulate others, "with or without recourse to solid grounding in historical materials, the struggle to control the image of the society through control of the interpretation of its cultural history goes on, *and it is part of the struggle to control the future of the society itself*" [emphasis in original].[26]

The U.S. Virgin Islands, though not aspiring to nationhood,[27] shares a history of exploitation, colonialism, and slavery with its sister islands in the Caribbean and likewise has a need to fashion its national identity and determine its cultural history. Its need for access to its archives touches the fundamental reasons for creating and keeping records.

ORAL TRADITION

Any understanding of the value of records to a record-keeping community must also consider the place of oral traditions in creating collective memory.

Oral tradition forms a vital part of the collective memory of many former colonial areas, such as the U.S. Virgin Islands, and often may be discovered, enhanced, or even reconstructed through clues in the written record. The access to written records also affects the ability to understand certain types of oral traditions, such as the significance of folk songs and stories, descriptions of events, and celebrations. Both the oral and the written memory operate in a symbiotic if not necessarily equal relationship to one another, augmenting and enhancing each other depending on the weight each is given within a society.

Considering the transition from oral to written records on an ancient-to-modern continuum, it becomes evident that each age confronts a similar dichotomy, though in vastly different relationships and proportions. Classicist Rosalind Thomas ponders the interchanging relationship between orality and literacy in Athens when, in examining literacy of the fourth and fifth centuries B.C., she writes, "We are forced to think again about the nature of literacy, the role of written record and communication by word of mouth and the interaction rather than the distinction between the two."[28] This point is also made by Michael Clanchy when considering the shift from an oral society to a literate one many centuries later in medieval England.[29] Similarly, in the twentieth century, a Nigerian educator suggests that "literate societies appear to rely on written records but do make recourse to oral history for historical information of recent vintage. For African societies, oral tradition, oral history and written records constitute a unified mode of historical consciousness."[30]

African archivists maintain that in many of their strongly oral societies, oral traditions assume some archival qualities. At a 1994 Pan-African Conference presentation, an archivist from the University of Ibadan pointed out that not only were nonliterate Africans conscious of their past and had their own systems of keeping records but that their oral traditions also constituted their archives. He explained that "these traditions are not just a mere recital by word of mouth of remembered history of a people," but that they also preserve the values and ideals of the society. Oral tradition provides records that have validity on all matters, as demonstrated even today in our customary courts. Cases of land, marriage, divorce, and so on are often determined on the basis of oral evidence.[31]

However, even in orally dominant societies, written records also have a valuable part to play. A Nigerian historian observes that although

the bulk of the primary historical source material of African history, in the form of oral testimonies, oral traditions, languages, rituals and other aspects of cultural life, and material artifact, both organic and inorganic, are not generally regarded as the responsibility of the archives. . . . the archives are crucial institutions in the formation and development of our historical consciousness because of the special significance of written records in historical reconstruction.[32]

The need to consider both oral traditions and written records is particularly relevant when considering the case of the U.S. Virgin Islands. Unlike many colonized areas—such as Africa or India, which had flourishing societies with clearly defined cultures and traditions for thousands of years before modern colonization and for whom that period of colonization forms only a tiny, though often devastating, part of a vast history—there is not even evidence of an existing Amerindian society in the Virgin Islands immediately previous to the time of Danish colonization in 1664.[33] The 250 years of colonialism, therefore, represent a substantial and formative period of Virgin Islands history. The written communications of the colonizer and the oral traditions of thousands of enslaved Africans brought to the colony existed side by side for two and a half centuries. Both are vital to understanding the history of that colonial past. Equally significant is the fact that the Danish colonizers did not share their language with the colonized,[34] even though Danish was the official language of all government and court records.[35] Enslaved Africans on St. Thomas and St. John developed a Creole language known as Negerhollands or Dutch Creole, while English became the lingua franca of trade and commerce. The lack of a common language presented additional obstacles for the colonized population, both in initially creating records and later in accessing them.

Despite the language exclusion created by the Danish colonizers, and the fact that "the slaves themselves were, by the nature of the institution of slavery, virtually barred from writing down their experiences and feelings and their reactions toward the situation in which they had been placed within the plantation society,"[36] both written evidence and oral tradition can offer perspectives on a shared past. From this perspective, folktales and folk songs may be considered as much repositories of historical and cultural evidence as are more formal records.

A Virgin Islands folklorist also points to the discrepancy between written and oral folk traditions, stressing that even though many of the folktales are written down, nuances in the physical movements and performance of the storyteller "make the full story come alive."[37] In her research on folkstory performance in the Virgin Islands, she urges thinking about the Virgin Islands tradition of storytelling as "not just a collection of simple folkstories but . . . a process, a creative/aesthetic performance process, involving the storyteller, the folkstories, the participants, and the setting through which it is generated and carried out in the community."[38] Songs are often interspersed within stories, which adds to their physical aspects. She explains that "long ago, the stories were told to educate the children, to learn about the history and values of the islands. . . . Today, even if the stories are not serving the same purpose, the children love to hear them and enjoy them, but most importantly they learn about their history and culture through them." When asked whether folktales carried messages beyond the actual stories, specifically whether they conveyed historical lessons, the folklorist refers to a popular tale called "A Boar Hog wid Gol' Teeth," a story about a fat and ugly white boar hog who disguises himself as a wealthy farmer and courts a young girl who will marry only a suitor with gold teeth. A small boy sees through the disguise and exposes it by playing a magic tune on his flute. The story makes fun of the class pretensions of the girl as well as of aspects of plantation life in which "a gentleman is a boarhog."[39] Within the folktale there are many historical references that give some idea of the environment, how people lived, what they did, and what they thought of each other.

For important historical events, however, a song alone would often tell the story because, as the folklorist suggests, "folk stories took on a completely different aura and these songs, the events were so historic and so important that the people did not want to put them into a make-believe component." The mockery and humor that were integral to folktales, in which animals often assumed human characteristics, may have been an effective way to teach moral behavior but were not considered an appropriate way to celebrate heroes. Virgin Islands oral tradition is filled with such heroic, history-telling songs as "Queen Mary," a popular favorite with musical groups and schoolchildren today, which celebrates the courageous and semi-mythical woman, Mary Thomas, who led the "Fireburn," the St. Croix Labor Revolt of 1878.

> Queen Mary, ah where you gon' go burn?
> Queen Mary, ah where you gon' go burn?
> Don't ask me nothin' 'tall
> Just geh me de match and oil,
> Bassin Jailhouse, ah deh de money dey.
>
> [Queen Mary, where are you going to burn?
> Queen Mary, where are you going to burn?
> Don't ask me anything at all
> Just get me the match and oil,
> Bassin Jailhouse, that's where the money is.][40]

ARCHIVES, ACCESS, AND COLLECTIVE MEMORY

Geographer Kenneth Foote warns of the danger in "assuming that collective memory is invested in any single type of human institution, such as the archives." He points out that the collective, interdependent nature of institutional memory "implies that the cultural role of the archives is hard to isolate from the contributions of other institutions and traditions."[41] Certainly this has proven to be true in attempting to reconstruct the colonial history of the Virgin Islands, in which oral traditions passed down by the slaves and their descendents and written records of Danish administrators offer divergent and often competing versions of historical events. Although the interdependent nature of sources suggests that all sides of the colonial coin are essential elements in forging and reconciling memory, much of the memory that has coalesced around historiography and commemoration in the Virgin Islands also illustrates that in the absence of documentary records, other forces become prominent in memory formation. The song of Queen Mary and the Fireburn, for example, looms large in Crucian historical and cultural consciousness though neither authenticated nor disproven through scholarship.[42]

In the face of these varied interdependent sources, are there relationships between archives and record-keeping communities that enable archivists to play a role in forging community memory? Most archivists would agree that the nurturing of collective memory has always been a central theme in the archival construct. When then International Council on Archives President Jean-Pierre Wallot coined the metaphor "houses of memory" in 1991, he referred to the "treasures of our past contained within archival institutions," where, he maintained, archivists are the holders of the "keys to collective memory."[43] Wallot suggested that archives can be both physical spaces and memory spaces. As physical spaces, they house their contents; as memory spaces, they are the containers of the collective memory of their creators as well as of their users and interpreters. As both physical and memory spaces they may stand as symbolic representations of particular values or ideas.

Certain principles of archival practice also reinforce both the physical and the memory aspects of the historical records that are maintained in archives, specifically the principles of custody and provenance. Archival custody, defined as the legal and physical control of records by an archival institution, has been fundamental to archival practice since the late nineteenth century.[44] In the last quarter of the twentieth century it has been the subject of often acrimonious debate as the archives community grapples with custody dilemmas posed by the proliferation of records and the increasing variety of formats. Of more urgency may be the dilemmas of communities and groups long denied full participation in defining their place in history, who increasingly recognize that possessing memory requires owning access to historical records, the facilitators of memory. The principle of archival custody is of immediate relevance in considering the case of the Virgin Islands, where the custodial claims of both Denmark and the United States took precedence over the historical needs of the native population. Removing the records from the islands also removed the possibilities of access for all but a few.

Examination of the archival situations of postcolonial societies, such as the U.S. Virgin Islands, indicates that decisions of record ownership made without full consideration of the access needs of the creating body may pose burdensome and sometimes insurmountable obstacles for these entities as they endeavor to grapple with their past. The existence of these obstacles jeopardizes and calls into question the validity of the entire custodial role. Expanding conventional ideas of archival custody so that access (rather than physical control) plays a central role in fulfilling the custodial obligation

would take these postcolonial dilemmas fully into account. It might also hold
the colonizer accountable and liable for providing reasonable access. Because
the construction of collective memory, and thereby collective identity, by
nations, communities, or groups of people depends on their ability to confront and understand their history, access is integral to the custody of historical records.

This study of the archives of the former Danish West Indies analyzes a community that for reasons relating both to its colonial status and to its sale to the
United States in 1917, has little ownership of its own history. In investigating
the extent to which historical records are essential ingredients in enabling the
Virgin Islands community to create its collective memory and consolidate its
identity, the following chapters will focus on various ways in which this community is forming its memory and the part played by historical records. From
an archival standpoint, this investigation also raises questions about whether
the principles of provenance and custody as generally interpreted and applied
by archivists are often too narrowly constructed to accommodate the complex
relations between historical records and the communities that produce them.

Chapter 2 presents the story of the Virgin Islands, its records, their creation, and their removal within both the Danish West Indian and American
contexts. Through interviews, analysis of commemorations, and examina-
tions of historiography, chapters 3 and 4 look at the forces affecting the
formation of community memory in the Virgin Islands today and the tensions
that have developed around contested and competing memories. The final
chapter draws on discussions with Virgin Islanders as well as historical and
archival methodologies to suggest ways that the oral and written traditions
of the Virgin Islands and other postcolonial communities can be reconciled,
both by archivists and others, to shine light into the "dark hole" of history
and return the ownership of the past to its rightful communities.

NOTES

1. Transfer Day is a public holiday in the Virgin Islands. Observed annually on
March 31, the celebration generally includes a reenactment of the original ceremony
on St. Thomas.

2. Marc Bloch, *The Historian's Craft* (New York: Vintage Books, 1953), 61. For
the interpretation of this phrase within the context of the records of a primarily oral
colonial society, I am indebted to the work of Danish anthropologist Karen Fog Olwig.
See her discussion of archival evidence in *Cultural Adaptation and Resistance on St.
John: Three Centuries of Afro-Caribbean Life* (Gainesville: University of Florida Press,
1987) and " 'Witnesses in Spite of Themselves': Reconstructing Afro-Caribbean Culture in the Danish West Indian Archives," *Scandinavian Economic History Review* 32
(1984): 61–76.

3. Tom Nesmith, ed. *Canadian Archival Studies and the Rediscovery of Provenance*
(Metuchen, N.J.: Scarecrow Press, 1993), 17.

4. Tom Nesmith, "Seeing Archives: Postmodernism and the Changing Intellectual Place of Archives," *American Archivist* 65 (Spring/Summer 2002): 35.

5. Jack Goody, *The Interface Between the Written and the Oral* (Cambridge: Cambridge University Press, 1987), 19.

6. Henri-Jean Martin, *The History and Power of Writing* (Chicago: University of Chicago Press, 1994), 27.

7. Ernst Posner in *Archives in the Ancient World* (Cambridge, Mass.: Harvard University Press, 1972), 3–70, identifies the Assyrians as the earliest record keepers; however, the birth of records themselves has been traced by Henri-Jean Martin to 3500 B.C. and the use of bullae or clay seals as signifiers for "registering transactions and managing an accumulated wealth," see his *History and the Power of Writing*, 9.

8. Terry Cook, "Electronic Records, Paper Minds: The Revolution in Information Management and Archives in the Post-Custodial and Post-Modernist Era," *Archives and Manuscripts* 22 (November 1994): 302.

9. Maier discusses this in the section "In English Ways," in her *American Scripture, Making the Declaration of Independence* (New York: Vintage Books, 1997), 50–59.

10. Benedict Anderson, *Imagined Communities: Reflections on the Origin and Spread of Nationalism*, rev. ed. (London: Verso, 1995).

11. Posner, *Archives in the Ancient World*, 1.

12. Rosalind Thomas, *Literacy and Orality in Ancient Greece* (Cambridge: Cambridge University Press, 1992), 88–93; M. T. Clanchy, *From Memory to Written Record, England 1066–1307* (Oxford: Blackwell, 1993), 44–74.

13. Anderson in *Imagined Communities* analyzes those elements, including the invention of printing, that create a sense of nationalism.

14. Ernst Posner, *American State Archives* (Chicago: University of Chicago Press, 1964), 11.

15. Nicholas Falco, "The Empire State's Search in European Archives," *American Archivist* 32 (April 1969): 110.

16. *Documania* was coined by David van Tassel in *Recording America's Past: An Interpretation of the Development of Historical Studies in America, 1607–1884* (Chicago: University of Chicago Press, 1960).

17. van Tassel, *Recording America's Past*, 103; Posner, *American State Archives*, 10–13; Richard J. Cox, "Other Atlantic States: Delaware, Florida, George, Maryland, New Jersey and South Carolina," in *Historical Consciousness in the Early Republic: The Origins of State Historical Societies, Museums and Collections, 1791–1861* (Chapel Hill: North Caroliniana Society, 1995), 106–7.

18. Cox, "Other Atlantic States," 112.

19. Bruce G. Wilson, "Bringing Home Canada's Archival Heritage: The London Office of the Public Archives of Canada, 1872–1986," *Archivaria* 21 (Winter 1985–86): 38.

20. V. S. Naipaul, *The Middle Passage: Impressions of Five Societies—British, French and Dutch—in the West Indies and South America* (New York: Macmillan, 1963), 29.

21. Waldemar Westergaard, *The Danish West Indies Under Company Rule, 1671–1754. With a Supplementary Chapter, 1755–1917* (New York: Macmillan, 1917), vi.

22. Walcott is from the island of St. Lucia; Trouillot is from Haiti.

23. Derek Walcott, "A Frowsty Fragrance," *New York Review of Books*, June 15, 2000, 61.

24. Michel-Rolph Trouillot, *Silencing the Past: Power and the Production of History* (Boston: Beacon Press, 1995), 51.

25. I am grateful to Daniel Hopkins, professor at the University of Missouri, Kansas City, for sharing his observations on Virgin Islands history.

26. Wendell Bell and Ivar Oxaal, *Decisions of Nationhood: Political and Social Development in the British Caribbean* (Denver: Denver University Press, 1964), 61.

27. The U.S. Congress declared the Virgin Islands an unincorporated territory of the United States in 1954. Over the past thirty years, four constitutional conventions and two referenda have been held in the Virgin Islands to allow the local community to write its own constitution and declare its preferred status, but all have been unsuccessful. Although independence has always been a status option, it has never garnered a significant number of votes. For a comprehensive discussion of the status issue as it relates to the territories of the United States, including the Virgin Islands, see Arnold H. Liebowitz, *Defining Status: A Comprehensive Analysis of United States Territorial Relations* (Netherlands: Kluwer, 1989).

28. Rosalind Thomas, *Oral Tradition and Written Record in Classical Athens* (Cambridge University Press, 1989), 2.

29. The coexistence of orality and literacy is a motif throughout Clanchy, *From Memory to Written Record, England 1066–1307.*

30. B. Aleybeleye, "Oral Archives in Africa: Their Nature, Value and Accessibility," *International Library Review* 17 (1985): 420.

31. Bolanle Awe, "The Concept of Archives in Africa: A Preliminary Survey," *Janus* 1 (1996): 73.

32. Yusufu Bala Usman, "The Significance of Primary Historical Source Material for African Unity and Integration," *Janus* 1 (1966): 16.

33. There is strong archeological evidence of an early Taino and Carib Indian presence in the Virgin Islands. Indians met Christopher Columbus when he sailed into Salt River, St. Croix, in 1493 (Columbus and his men also killed several of the Indians who came to meet them, an event known in Virgin Islands lore as "the Bloody Encounter"). As recently as July 1998, a Taino artifact was uncovered on St. John during an archeological dig at the possible site of an Indian village ("St. John Dig Yields Artifact," *Virgin Islands Daily News,* 17 July, 1998, 1–2). The Indian population had disappeared from the area of the Virgin Islands by the time the first Danish colonists arrived in 1665.

34. Even at the height of their colonial empire, Danish, the language of officialdom, was never passed on to the colonized. Dutch and then English rapidly became the lingua franca of commerce in the colonies. By 1830, English was being taught in the slave primary schools. See Neville A. T. Hall, *Slave Society in the Danish West Indies: St. Thomas, St. John and St. Croix* (Jamaica: University of the West Indies Press, 1992), 17–18.

35. Even when court testimony was given in English, it was translated by the clerk of the court into Danish, so that the surviving official record is Danish.

36. Olwig, *Cultural Adaptation and Resistance on St. John,* 8.

37. I am indebted to Virgin Islands folklorist, musician, and educator Lois Hassell Habteyes for sharing her insights, experience, and knowledge during an interview on St. Thomas in March 1999.

38. Lois Hassel Habteyes, "Tell Me a Story About Long Time: A Study of the

Folkstory Performance Tradition in the United States Virgin Islands" (Ph.D. diss., University of Illinois at Urbana-Champaign, 1985), 2.

39. Habteyes, "Tell Me a Story About Long Time," 46, 134.

40. The author of "Queen Mary" is unknown. The song is collected in Marvin E. Williams, editor and compiler, *Yellow Cedars Blooming: An Anthology of Virgin Islands Poetry* (U.S. Virgin Islands: Humanities Council, 1998), 32. I thank Calvin and Fiamma Bastian for their help with the translation.

41. Kenneth E. Foote, "To Remember and Forget: Archives, Memory and Culture," *American Archivist* 53 (Summer 1990): 380. In a subsequent book, *Shadowed Ground: America's Landscapes of Violence and Tragedy* (Austin: University of Texas Press, 1997), Foote builds on the concept of collective memory as an aggregate of a variety of types of documentation when he explores the role of monuments, memorials, buildings, and the landscape itself in interpreting and constructing memories of tragic events.

42. A Crucian is a person born on St. Croix; a St. Thomian, on St. Thomas.

43. Jean-Pierre Wallot, "Building a Living Memory for the History of Our Present: New Perspectives on Archival Appraisal," *Journal of the Canadian Historical Association* 2 (1991): 282.

44. Although the practice of making and keeping records dates back to the time of ancient Assyrian civilization, modern archival theory did not begin to develop until the late nineteenth century, with the 1898 appearance of the *Manual for the Arrangement and Description of Archives* by Dutch archivists S. Muller, J. A Feith, and R. Fruin.

2

HOW THE VIRGIN ISLANDS LOST ITS MEMORY

INTRODUCTION

In 1696, church registers created by French Catholic missionaries on St. Croix were removed to Haiti when the French colonizers evacuated that island and reassigned its missionaries. Once in Haiti, the records were kept in a storeroom containing rock salt, which caused rapid deterioration. When the priests discovered the damage, they copied whatever they could read into Haitian registers that were removed to France sometime during the Haitian revolution of 1798. The records of St. Croix remained hidden within these registers until they were rediscovered by archivists in Paris in the twentieth century. Although this was likely the first incidence of records removal from the Virgin Islands, it was not the last. Indeed, this small vignette is only a precursor to a series of records removals that essentially deprived the Virgin Islands community of its historical memory.[1]

The archival records sent from the Virgin Islands to Denmark following the transfer of the islands in 1917 together with records sent to the National Archives of the United States in the 1930s through the 1950s represented nearly three hundred years worth of record keeping. This odyssey took place within the context of colonialism, in which the colonizing powers that created the records then removed them to archives in their own countries. How this came about is crucial to appreciating the impact that records loss had on the community that remained behind, a loss suggesting that the evolution of any community is indivisible from the records it creates.

A BRIEF HISTORY OF THE UNITED STATES VIRGIN ISLANDS

The Virgin Islands archipelago—consisting of the three islands of St. Thomas, St. Croix, and St. John and hundreds of smaller islands and cays—is located approximately 1,000 miles from the southernmost tip of the coast of Florida.[2] This small group of tropical islands lies at the top of the arc of the Lesser Antilles, a chain of islands stretching down the Caribbean Sea to Trinidad and the coast of South America. Characterized in 1918 as "the place which is on the way to every other place,"[3] the Virgin Islands were at the hub of sea routes extending north to Europe and North America and south to other islands in the Caribbean from the seventeenth to the nineteenth centuries. From its early settlement in the seventeenth century as both a trading entrepôt and a plantation site to its twentieth-century purchase for military strategic purposes and its renown as a tourist destination today, the history of the Virgin Islands has been profoundly influenced by its geographical location.

The separation and physical dissimilarity of the islands may be their most outstanding features. All are volcanic extrusions; although St. Thomas and St. John are completely mountainous, St. Croix is generally flat, with hills at only one end of the island. St. Thomas and St. John are three miles apart, and St. Croix is forty miles south of St. Thomas.

When Christopher Columbus "discovered" the Virgin Islands in 1493 on his second voyage, they were inhabited by Carib Indians who met and resisted Columbus and his men at Salt River on November 14, 1493, on the island he named Santa Cruz (later known as St. Croix). A few days later, while sailing through a cluster of smaller islands to the north, Columbus named them Las Once Mil Virgines (the 11,000 virgins) in honor of the legend of St. Ursula and her 11,000 martyred virgins, because of their number and (it is claimed) to exaggerate the magnitude of his discovery in the eyes of his royal patrons, Ferdinand and Isabella of Spain.[4]

Through Columbus's discovery, the Spanish claimed the right to colonize the islands of the Lesser Antilles. But they never did, preferring the larger islands of the Greater Antilles and leaving the Virgin Islands for the lesser European colonizers to squabble over. The initial ferocity of the Indians possibly made the Spaniards wary of further involvement. However, by the time of the first Dutch settlements on St. Croix around 1625, the Indian population had completely disappeared, and the early colonists found uninhabited lands on all three of the islands. Historians have speculated that the lack of a native population as a source of labor may have been one factor that encouraged the development of the slave trade.

Before its purchase by Denmark from France in 1733, St. Croix had changed hands numerous times as competing European powers (French, Dutch, and English) vied with one another to increase their Caribbean holdings and trade routes. St. Thomas, on the other hand, was first settled by

Denmark in 1665 and, except for eight years of English conquest between 1807 and 1815, remained in Danish hands for 250 years. St. John, claimed by Denmark in 1683, was not settled until 1718.

Early settlement in St. Thomas was sponsored by the Danish West India Company, a commercial venture chartered by the Danish Crown to develop trading areas for Denmark in the West Indies. Although the first colony established there in 1665 failed due to attacks by both English privateers and fatal disease, St. Thomas's potential as a trading center and plantation colony had become evident to the Danes early on, and a second attempt at colonization in 1672 was successful. However, due to rampant yellow fever and malaria as well as limited opportunities for individual profit, it was difficult for the company to find willing settlers. They were forced to fall back on indentured immigrants and prisoners for labor. The poor quality of the laborers[5] as well as the mortality rate also influenced the rapid development of the slave trade because a reliable source of labor was needed if the plantations were to become profitable.[6]

The colonization of St. Thomas coincided with the outbreak of war between the Netherlands on one side and Britain and France on the other. Consequently, a large number of settlers from the Dutch island possessions fled to the relative safety and neutrality of St. Thomas. This sizable Dutch population—as well as German, English, and French colonists who migrated from other islands to the new colony—were welcomed by the Danes, not only because they boosted the population but also because they brought expertise in plantation agriculture. From the outset, then, St. Thomas was a polyglot of nationalities and languages. Although the Danes were the owners of the colony, they were at no time the majority population during their 250 years of colonial rule, nor was Danish ever the primary language of the populace. Initially it was Dutch and, later, English.[7]

In 1673, the king of Denmark granted the Danish West India Company a royal charter to assume control of the Guinea Company, a recently formed Danish slave trade operation on the coast of West Africa. The need for labor on the St. Thomas plantations had become acute. Both the advantages and the profitability of slave labor and the ensuing trade were so great that by 1715 the white population of St. Thomas was still only 547, whereas the enslaved African population numbered 3,042 on 160 plantations.[8] Despite the lucrative possibilities of the African slave trade, however, the newly renamed Danish West India and Guinea Company continued to operate at a loss due to the costs of colonization, debts incurred by planters that were underwritten by the company, and losses of slave ships. The charter had given the company the right to colonize St. Thomas and any other uninhabited island. St. John, which had been claimed for the company in 1675, seemed well suited for plantation development. Accordingly, and in spite of opposition by the English who controlled the nearby Leeward Islands, a colony was established on St. John in 1718.

Still seeking to revive a continually declining economy, the company then sought to purchase St. Croix from the French. St. Croix had already experienced a violent and complex history. Since the first Spanish settlement in 1625, it had been occupied by several European nations. Following the defeat of the Spaniards, French settlers took possession in 1650. As French colonies in the West Indies fell into decline and after a brief ownership by the Order of the Knights of Malta, St. Croix was transferred directly to the French Crown. Subsequently the colony was abandoned in 1696. The Danish West India and Guinea Company purchased the island from France in 1733. In spite of this expansion, the company still did not make a profit. In 1754, at the urging of the planters, the Danish West India and Guinea Company, which had been operating at a financial loss since its inception, dissolved itself in favor of the Danish government. The Danish Crown assumed administration of the islands.

In 1733, the African slave population instigated a violent rebellion on St. John that, though harshly repressed, temporarily discouraged further plantation development. Many of the St. John planters moved to St. Croix. St. Thomas, with its mountainous terrain, had never been well suited to agriculture, but its wide, deep, natural harbor encouraged rapid development as a major port and trading center, although it also attracted pirates. St. Croix, flat and three times the area of St. Thomas, was perfectly suited to a plantation economy and became the focus of Danish colonial agricultural development. Because of this plantation development with its total dependence on chattel slavery, St. Croix also became the center of the slave economy in the Danish West Indies. Although St. Thomas saw the gradual growth of a free black population and the development of an artisan class, St. Croix plantation owners, completely dependent on a free and ample labor force, increasingly tried to protect their investments through a series of harsh slave laws. St. Croix, therefore, became the center of unrest and rebellion in the Danish West Indies and was where the social reforms leading to emancipation and beyond were fomented.

A 1792 Danish royal edict mandated that the transatlantic trade in African slaves between West Africa and the Danish West Indies must cease by January 1, 1803. The intervening ten years would be used to encourage primarily St. Croix plantations to build up a labor force that could continue to prosper by reproducing itself.[9] The planters, however, did not initiate the accommodations and reforms within the slave community that would have enabled this to take place. Slave mortality, which had always been a major factor in an economy that never really met its profit potential, continued to rise. However, despite bitter opposition by the planters and efforts to extend the deadline, the edict went into effect as decreed. In 1803 Denmark officially abolished its slave trade, becoming the first European power to do so. In 1803 the number of enslaved Africans recorded in St. Croix was 27,161. The white population had always been small in proportion to the black population, and by 1803 was just over 6 percent.[10]

In 1833, enslaved Africans in the colonies of the British Caribbean were emancipated by order of the British Parliament. This event has been viewed by historians as a turning point for the slaves of the Danish West Indies. The island of Tortola, a British colony, lay only a few miles beyond St. John, and news of the British emancipation undoubtedly had a strong impact.[11] Additionally, a number of other factors—including the opening of publicly supported slave schools, the missionary influence, the increased socialization of the now primarily Creole slave population, and humanitarian movements in Europe—forced the Danish government to recognize that emancipation of the slaves was both inevitable and imminent. The British government had compensated its planters for the loss of their slaves, but the Danish government was unable to do the same and so attempted to find another source of amelioration. In the Free Birth Proclamation of 1847 the government conferred freedom on all slaves born after that date and set a date for general emancipation in twelve years. This proclamation became a catalyst for freedom and gave new urgency to the drive for emancipation because the "adult slave population would not postpone their inheritance of a freedom to which they felt that their children were no more legitimate heirs than themselves."[12]

On July 3, 1848, slaves on St. Croix initiated a bloodless rebellion that resulted in the immediate emancipation of all enslaved in the Danish West Indies. However, employment conditions for the newly freed were so bad and wages so minimal that living conditions were little better (and often worse) than they had been under slavery. These agricultural laborers finally revolted in 1878. Descriptively known as the Fireburn, this organized rebellion purportedly led by a woman, Queen Mary, resulted in the destruction of both plantations and lives but led to the initiation of labor reforms. It also sounded the initial death knell for the plantation economy of St. Croix.

In the latter half of the nineteenth century, the steady demise of sugar cane in favor of the beet as a sugar source, the simultaneous decline of St. Thomas as the shipping center of the Caribbean, and a series of natural disasters contributed to the decreasing economic viability of the islands. Denmark increasingly saw them as financial and social burdens and so were receptive to an offer of purchase from the United States in 1867. This initiative, fueled primarily by Secretary of State William Seward, who saw the need for the United States to protect itself on all sides after the Civil War, failed for lack of congressional support.[13] A second attempt at purchase in 1892 was not ratified by the Danish parliament. A final agreement was reached in 1916 and the Danish West Indies was sold to the United States for $25 million and renamed the United States Virgin Islands.

The U.S. Department of the Navy was given the task of administering the new territory through a naval governor appointed by the president. Local agitation and unrest forced the United States to grant citizenship to the inhabitants in 1927, reinterpreting a clause in the transfer treaty that had been deliberately ambiguous.[14] In 1931, prompted by increasing dissatisfaction with a generally racist naval administration,[15] the territory was transferred to a civilian administration under the Department of the Interior.

In 1936, Congress passed the Organic Act, which for the first time outlined a measure of self-government for the Virgin Islands. Although the governor was still appointed by the president, locally elected municipal councils on each island and a legislative assembly gave the population more control over its own governance. However, not until the Revised Organic Act of 1954, which extended self-government provisions to include the election of a unicameral legislature, was the status of the Virgin Islands as an "unincorporated territory" defined.[16] In 1968 Congress passed the Elective Governor Act, which allowed Virgin Islanders to elect their own governor. Currently, the Virgin Islands, although remaining under the oversight of the Office of Territories in the Department of the Interior, elects all its local officials and passes its own locally applicable legislation. However, residents cannot vote in national elections and have a nonvoting delegate representing them in Congress. Despite four constitutional conventions and two status referenda held between 1964 and 1994, the Virgin Islands electorate has so far opted not to change its status. There has been no recommendation to Congress for a constitution, and the U.S. Virgin Islands remains an unincorporated territory of the United States.[17]

THE MAKING OF THE DANISH WEST INDIAN RECORDS

From its earliest settlement, the population of the Danish West Indies was heterogeneous, and demographics indicate that from the introduction of slavery into the islands, African peoples, enslaved or free, were always in the majority and played a central role in the earliest records of the settlements. Whether involved in transactions or as the actual transactions themselves, they were integral to the life of the colony. Although the enslaved Africans created few written records, to a great extent the records reflect their lives, and the conditions of enslavement form a central touchstone in the collective memory of Virgin Islanders today.[18]

Beginning with the early days of the Danish West India Company in the late seventeenth century, record keeping was an important part of daily activity. Following the sale of the company to the Danish government, a complex colonial bureaucracy ensured the production and proliferation of quantities of records. Careful records of all transactions and events were kept both by the Colonial Offices in Denmark and by the colonial government offices in the Danish West Indies. The Danes were notoriously meticulous and assiduous record keepers. Their records not only give a very rich, complete, and detailed account of over 250 years of colonial development but also provide extensive documentation about colonial societies, slavery, and the slave trade.

The records created during Crown rule between 1754 and 1917 were considerable and diverse in both the islands and Denmark. The records from this period are divided into two groups—those of the central government created in Denmark, known as the Danish Central Administration Records, and those created in the colony, known as the West Indian Local Archives.[19] Copies of many of the administrative records created in the Danish West Indies were sent to Denmark and vice versa. But the records of minor local authorities, such as harbormasters and judges, generally only exist in the West Indian Local Archives in Copenhagen or in Washington, with a small amount remaining in the islands. Even so, this duplication often means that a copy of a record can be found somewhere.

The language of the records has also had a major impact on their accessibility. Because the official language of the colonies was Danish, all official records were written in that language, even though, as already discussed, Danish was not the lingua franca of the majority of the population. The enslaved Africans on St. Thomas and St. John developed Dutch Creole, or Negerhollands, a language combining Dutch and African influences. Linguists have speculated that the Dutch language influence, though strongly reinforced through the predominance of Dutch planters on St. Thomas and St. John, may have been initially acquired on the coast of Africa.[20] Moravian missionaries in the Danish West Indies further reinforced Dutch Creole as the language of the slaves by publishing a Bible and hymnals in this language, as a way of both educating and proselytizing.[21] On St. Croix, due to the predominance of English planters, an English-based Creole developed. The Danish language was not taught to the populace. The only early source of education for the slaves was that offered by Moravian missionaries. When the Danish government did institute a school system for the slaves in the 1840s, instruction was in English.

In spite of the fact that the majority of the population could not understand the language, official records continued to be produced in Danish until 1917; however, beginning in 1860 English translations of official notices were made available through the local newspapers. Even court testimony taken in English or any other language was immediately translated by the clerk and transcribed into Danish.

The lack of any Danish-language tradition significantly affected the ability of later generations of Virgin Islanders to read the records of their own history. Moreover, the reluctance (or inability) to pass the language on to the colonial population stands as a significant commentary for at least one historian on the purely commercial objectives of Danish colonialism. Neville Hall notes that "colonization implied more than territorial claim and a body of laws. It called for a significant body of one's nationals, sharing one's customs and values and, above all, language. Without these, the objectives of colonization . . . could not be realized."[22]

THE DANISH GOVERNMENT AND THE RECORDS

In the mid-nineteenth century, colonial officials in the Danish West Indies became concerned about their local government records for several reasons: tropical climate and insects were causing rapid deterioration, and the moving of the government itself between buildings and islands with varying qualities of storage created disorder as well as uncertain storage conditions.[23] In addition to the tropical climate and the attendant insects and rodents, natural and political upheavals also created a climate of uncertainty for the records. A 1772 hurricane destroyed many pre-1755 records, and in 1848, during the emancipation rebellion, all the records in the Frederiksted, St. Croix, government offices (court and criminal records) were destroyed by an angry mob.[24] In 1801, when the St. Croix records were consolidated and moved to the Government House, they were put in order and essentially kept that way under the responsibility of a royal head clerk. It is also clear from such chroniclers as John Knox (1852), who frequently refers to the deteriorated condition of records, that although records were kept, they were not always kept well. In a telling description of record storage conditions, Governor Peter Hansen reports on a self-igniting fire in 1851 at Government House in St. Croix in which "it seems likely that some Lucifer-matches had been stored away, perhaps many years ago, on one of the worm-infested shelves among papers, and then mice, of which there are many in the offices, had gnawed on them, and the matches had then ignited."[25]

On St. Thomas, the situation was no better. Records were initially stored in the military Fort Christian under the supervision of the government-appointed secretary but then were moved to Government House.[26] Between 1823 and 1880 various measures were taken to protect them from insects, primarily by storing them in boxes coated with pitch, and they were moved around to different locations. Apparently, these locations "were in such condition that you could hardly have chosen better places if you had wanted them destroyed."[27] In the 1880s a salary was created to pay an attorney on St. Thomas to organize the local archives collection, and in 1894 the Danish government began to make attempts to bring the archives to Denmark.

The Danish National Archives, formerly known as the Royal Archives, was established in 1582 as the central repository for documents of importance to the Crown and the state. Not until passage of the Archives Law of 1889, however, were all the government archival institutions in the country unified and given the official name Rigsarkivet (Danish National Archives). In 1891 policies were instituted to enable transferring records from government agencies to the central archives, including those from the Danish overseas possessions.

Regardless of the regulations, however, local colonial officials were reluctant to send the records to Denmark on the grounds that should they be needed, they could not easily be retrieved. They could only be persuaded to part with those records created up to the early part of the nineteenth century. The Rigsarkivet made a list of the archival registers that they wanted sent using a cut-off date of 1848 and based on the premise that "it would be desirable that the older purely historical cases be gathered in the Rigsarkiv for information on the history of the colonies and personal biographies . . . partially to keep them safe, and partially to make them accessible to the student of history."[28] The anticipated sale of the islands also provided an impetus for sending the archives to Denmark.

In spite of prevarication by numerous colonial offices, the first transfer took place in 1893. This was followed by smaller transfers until 1921, when the bulk of the records were sent for deposit. The records of the Danish West India Company, some two hundred linear feet, had already been sent to the Royal Archives in 1754 upon the dissolution of the company.

In all, there are approximately four thousand linear shelf-feet of West Indian Archives in the Danish National Archives. Over half of these are the West Indian Local Archives or records created in the colonies. The remainder are records created in the colonial offices in Denmark.

THE RECORDS UNDER THE U.S. ADMINISTRATION

The convention between Denmark and the United States transferring the Danish West Indies to U.S. control in 1916 specifically included stipulations for the disposition of the archives and records. The third paragraph of Article 1 states:

In this cession shall also be included any government archives, records, papers or documents which relate to the cession or to the rights and property of the inhabitants of the Islands ceded, and which may now be existing either in the Islands ceded or in Denmark. Such archives and records shall be carefully preserved, and authenticated copies thereof, as may be required shall be at all times given to the United States Government or the Danish Government, as the case may be, or to such properly authorized persons as may apply for them.[29]

For Denmark, as they negotiated independence with their former possessions, it was normal practice to include a clause about archival materials in relationship to the administration of the ceded territories.[30] Conversely, as the United States acquired territories between 1803 and 1917, a clause relating to archives disposition was likewise included as in the treaties for the Louisiana Purchase, the purchase of Florida, and the 1898 annexation of Puerto Rico.

The archives provision in the Denmark/United States treaty, therefore, was standard practice on the part of both countries. The transfer of properties and the rights pertaining to them included transfer of the symbols of those properties, namely, the records of ownership. Custody of the records was regarded as essential to the ownership of the land. The 1916 treaty referencing the records existing in both the islands and Denmark specifically mentions the inhabitants as having rights to get copies of the records and recognizes the possibility of a reciprocal flow of records.

Although the aborted draft treaties of 1867 and 1902 referred to records existing in the islands only, they failed to mention any connection between the records and the inhabitants. They only envisioned a one-way records flow, from the United States to Denmark. The 1916 version, however, included records existing in both the islands and Denmark, specifically mentions the inhabitants as having rights to copies of the records, and recognizes the possibility of a reciprocal flow.

Whatever the advantages or disadvantages of this archives clause, what is clear is that the Americans paid little if any attention to it or the archives in the early years following the transfer. Perhaps, as archivist Ernst Posner has suggested, their failure to take custody of the records that were legally theirs was due at least partly to lack of competent advice by archivists.[31] More likely it was due to the urgency of the overwhelming clean-up task that the Americans were forced to undertake immediately on assuming control of the islands. Naval administration Governor James Oliver presented the grim reality in his first annual report to the Secretary of the Navy, writing that "the problems to be faced in the most elementary improvement of the present conditions in these islands with particular reference to sanitation, hygiene, public morality, finances, etc., are so many and so grave."[32] Hospitals, health, and sewage systems were in unspeakable condition. There was no water distribution system, a minimal and ineffective education system, no fire protection, and, worst of all, little employment for the population. Infant mortality was high, the economy depressingly low. Not surprisingly, the disposition of archives and records had no priority. In addition, the crucial fact that there was no national archive in the United States meant that there was no advocate for the records and no one to protect their interests.

Denmark stepped in to fill the vacuum. Once the impending sale became a reality and the Danes had an opportunity to study the archives clause, various Danish historical societies began to lobby their government to bring the records to the Danish National Archives. These groups, which included genealogists, biographers, and historians, sent a petition to the government urging the historical importance of preserving the documents. They recommended that because the records created before 1863 had lost their administrative importance, they needed to be brought to Denmark, and the remainder should be reviewed by archivists before final decisions were made.

The Danish government essentially agreed with this assessment. Accordingly, in 1919 they sent their archivist, Georg Saxild, to the Virgin Islands to negotiate for certain records to be sent to Denmark. On his arrival, however,

Saxild discovered that the navy had no interest in negotiating and allowed him to take whatever he wanted. In his report to the Danish government, he observes that "in the American administration there is next to no interest in archives. It was very clear that none of the American officials (the school principal, the military doctor, et al.) who visited me out of curiosity while I was working understood why I wanted all that 'rubbish' that I was going through."[33] Accordingly he spent several months, with local assistance, packing records in St. Thomas and St. Croix into wooden crates and arranging for shipment to Denmark. Saxild describes the records as being generally in disarray and stored in abominable conditions. Although he had carte blanche to take what he wanted, he generally confined himself to records before 1900; in his selection of records, he makes clear that he made many of his choices based on the perceived need of the Danes for their history.[34] He scrupulously observed the terms of the treaty by exempting property records, such as deed and mortgage books, and some legal and financial records, thereby respecting the needs of the propertied classes that remained in the islands.

Some of the frustrations at finding records in disarray as well as in a foreign language are expressed in the naval governor's early annual reports. The 1917 report, discussing the very poor conditions in the government's administrative offices, complains that "there is no place to file correspondence and records except on shelves which are congested with the accumulation of many years." The law books were all in Danish and had not been translated into English. On the other hand, by 1918, the surveying records, also in Danish and found in a "more or less haphazard manner," were being translated and organized by navy personnel.[35]

In 1936, the newly established National Archives of the United States, finally acknowledging its claim to and responsibility for the records, sent a Danish-speaking archivist, Harold Larson, to the Virgin Islands as part of the Survey of Federal Records Project.[36] By that time, the Virgin Islands had been administratively transferred from the Department of the Navy to the Office of Territories in the Department of the Interior. Larson was given a leave of absence and was appointed as a Special Assistant to Governor Lawrence Cramer, the civilian governor in the Virgin Islands, who had been appointed local administrator of the Works Progress Administration by President Franklin Roosevelt.

Larson stayed in the Virgin Islands from August 1936 to April 1937, employed five local assistants, and examined and selected Danish records for transfer to the custody of the National Archives. Though the majority of the records were created after the 1848 cut-off date set by the Danes, a number of them, particularly on St. Croix, date back to the seventeenth century. In his selection criteria, Larson excluded all records involving land titles and all that had been created after 1917, feeling that these should remain in the islands. His inventory lists material of historical significance as well as series dealing with a variety of topics, such as agriculture, social conditions, and local legislative and judicial records. He found the records in very poor physical condition—termite-ridden, brittle, and fragile. He suggests that problems for future researchers, in addition to the fragility, included the fact that the records were in Danish, that the older records used gothic script, and that the handwriting was often illegible. In the introduction to his preliminary inventory Larson takes note of the obligations implied under the archives clause in the treaty, writing, "the present accession was made with the understanding that the Government of the Virgin Islands or its representatives, upon request should be given all available information from these records." The entire accession, sent in three shipments, was 1,462 cubic feet or 1,260 linear feet.[37]

In 1942, the National Archives sent archivist Gaston Litton, a field representative for the agency who was surveying records in Panama, to the Virgin Islands, Puerto Rico, and the Canal Zone. His mission was to survey those federal records, report on their physical condition, and recommend dispositions and transfers to Washington.[38] Ensuing correspondence between Litton, officials at the National Archives, and Robert Lovett, government secretary and acting governor in the Virgin Islands, indicates that the survey was eagerly received by Lovett, who was anxious to transfer inactive Danish records to the safe keeping of the National Archives because the Virgin Islands had neither the facilities nor the staff to take care of them. However, the municipal councils on both St. Thomas/St. John and St. Croix were not as tractable and firmly resisted all suggestions that any of the legislative records be removed. Nonetheless, Litton (who recognized that many of the Danish records completed record series already at the National Archives) and Lovett were able to persuade many of the other local Virgin Islands offices to transfer their inactive files.

The hazards of sea travel in the Atlantic during World War II prevented any records transfers until the 1950s, when several smaller accessions of Danish records, one for 95 cubic feet and one for 309 cubic feet, were made in 1954 and 1955. These were primarily records dating from 1818 to 1917 but also included some post-1917 records. In 1953, the Virgin Islands governor again offered to send all the older records (except land records) to the National Archives. Those that were accepted were, like the 1937 accession, placed in Record Group 55 as part of the Natural Resources Records Branch. However, it seems clear from the accession lists that many of the legislative records were not transferred, even in the last accession in July 1959, when 204 cubic feet, made up of strictly post-1917 records with series going up to 1949, were sent to Washington.

Records pertaining to the Danish West Indies/Virgin Islands are found in a number of record groups in the National Archives, but the bulk of them are in Record Group 55. The older records are in such fragile condition that some of them are not available to users. Approximately 2,070 cubic feet of records were removed from the Virgin Islands to the National Archives.

These records generally complement (rather than duplicate) those in Denmark. Although the older records are in Danish, many of those, particularly Colonial Council records created from the mid-nineteenth century, are also in English. Together they complement and continue the rich history already deposited in Denmark.

In the late 1950s, the National Archives stopped taking records from the Virgin Islands, leaving this responsibility to the local government. Historical records remaining in the Virgin Islands are primarily the land records kept by the Recorder of Deeds as well as survey records in the Department of Public Works. Remnants of series, such as Police Court records and Municipal Council proceedings, are stored in the Division of Libraries and Archives on St. Thomas and St. Croix.

THE RECORDS AND THE VIRGIN ISLANDS

The loss of records in the Virgin Islands has itself become a part of the community's collective memory; researcher and citizen alike recognize that the bulk of their archives are not available to them. Myths and folklore abound concerning the disposition of the records. The author of a book on the historic architecture of the Virgin Islands, for example, insists that most official records were destroyed by "pirate raids, fires, change of flag and hurricanes," and that after the transfer, "many irreplaceable records were burned because they were in Danish, thus of no use to anyone."[39] In a similar disaster story, Danish historian Palle Lauring vividly writes of his experience as a colonial officer's son in St. Thomas, watching from the shore as the ocean turned white when packets of documents were thrown into the sea by government and military officials bitter over the failure of the 1902 sales negotiations. Lauring follows this up with an anecdote about American marines tossing away letter books and archives because they could not read them. As a Danish archivist points out, strictly observed Danish regulations regarding archives as well as the archives provision of the treaty make it highly unlikely that any of these incidents took place, although it is certainly possible that records were inadvertently destroyed during and after the transfer.[40]

Although these stories contribute to a community perception that many of its archives are lost, the wide recognition that the records of the Virgin Islands are not easily accessible is not a myth but is continually reinforced as educators, researchers, and the public seek to engage in history. Chapter 3 explores the problems and conflicts that Virgin Islanders encounter as they attempt to negotiate a historical narrative between elusive written sources and a strong, viable oral tradition.

NOTES

1. I am grateful to Aimery Caron for bringing this incident to my attention. For further description of the French colonial records on St. Croix, see Aimery Caron,

comp., *Inventory of French Documents Pertaining to the U.S. Virgin Islands, 1642–1737* (St. Thomas: Division of Libraries, Museums and Archaeological Services, 1978).

2. This brief account of the historical development of the Danish West Indies and the U.S. Virgin Islands draws from the following secondary sources: Isaac Dookhan, *A History of the Virgin Islands of the United States* (Essex, England: Caribbean Universities Press for the College of the Virgin Islands, 1974); Waldemar Westergaard, *The Danish West Indies Under Company Rule, 1671–1754* (New York: Macmillan, 1917); Neville A. T. Hall, *Slave Society in the Danish West Indies: St. Thomas, St. John and St. Croix,* ed. Barry Higman (Jamaica: University of the West Indies Press, 1992).

3. Theodore de Booy and John T. Faris, *The Virgin Islands: Our New Possessions and the British Islands* (Philadelphia: J. B. Lippincott, 1918; rpt., Westport, Conn.: Negro Universities Press, 1970), 54.

4. William W. Boyer, *America's Virgin Islands: A History of Human Rights and Wrongs* (Durham, N.C.: Carolina Academic Press, 1983), 2.

5. Dookhan, A History of the Virgin Islands of the United States, 48, 61. The difficulty of finding settlers initially forced to Danes to conscript prisoners as laborers on the plantations. Dookhan refers to the "low quality of the Danes who had been brought over as laborers," 61.

6. Both Boyer, *America's Virgin Islands,* 13, and Dookhan, *A History of the Virgin Islands of the United States,* 29, discuss the economic imperative for a labor force that drove the development of slavery. Boyer notes that the failure of Indian slavery, combined with the "limited servitude extracted from poor Europeans, including indentured servants and convicts, laid the base for the construction of African slavery" (13).

7. Hall, *Slave Society in the Danish West Indies.* In chapter 1, "Empire Without Dominion: The Danish West Indies, 1671–1848," Hall explores the language development in the context of the Danish minority population in the colonies.

8. Westergaard, *The Danish West Indies Under Company Rule,* 126.

9. For a detailed account of the abolition of the Danish slave trade, see Joseph Evans Loftin, "The Abolition of the Danish Atlantic Slave Trade," Ph.D. diss., Louisiana State University and Agricultural Mechanical College, 1977.

10. Svend E. Green-Pedersen, "The Scope and Structure of the Danish Negro Slave Trade," in *Bondsmen and Freedmen in the Danish West Indies, Scholarly Perspectives,* ed. George F. Tyson (St. Thomas: V.I. Humanities Council, 1996), 18.

11. Svend E. Holsoe, "The Beginning of the 1848 Emancipation Rebellion on St. Croix," in *Bondsmen and Freedmen in the Danish West Indies,* ed. George F. Tyson (St. Thomas: V.I. Humanities Council, 1996), 160. See also Hall, *Slave Society in the Danish West Indies,* 31.

12. Hall, *Slave Society in the Danish West Indies,* 207.

13. A detailed account from the American point of view of the negotiations leading up to the eventual sale in 1916 can be found in Charles Callan Tansill, *The Purchase of the Danish West Indies* (Gloucester, Mass.: Peter Smith, 1966). A partial account from the Danish point of view is presented in Erik Overgaard Pederson, "The Attempted Sale of the Danish West Indies to the United States of America, 1865–1870," Ph.D. diss., City University of New York, 1992.

14. The automatic granting of U.S. citizenship to Virgin Islanders was an important selling point in the negotiations for both the Danes and the Virgin Islanders; however, the treaty was ambiguous. The official U.S. interpretation was that the "inhabitants of the Virgin Islands had American nationality and were entitled to the protection of

the Government, but that they did not have the civil and political status of citizens" (Dookhan, *A History of the Virgin Islands of the United States,* 275).

15. The marked racial biases of the navy are acknowledged in every history text on the Virgin Islands that cover this period.

16. An "unincorporated territory belongs to the United States; is under the sovereignty of the United States; but is not part of the Union. Only the fundamental parts of the Constitution apply of their own force in unincorporated territories" (Paul M. Leary, ed., *Major Political and Constitutional Documents of the United States Virgin Islands, 1671–1991* [St. Thomas: University of the Virgin Islands, 1992], 349).

17. For in-depth analysis of the constitutional conventions, the status referenda, and the whole issue of status as it applied to all the U.S. territories, see Arnold Liebowitz, *Defining Status: A Comprehensive Analysis of United States Territorial Relations* (Dordrecht, Netherlands: Kluwer Law International, 1989), and Paul Leary, ed., *United States Virgin Islands Major Political Documents, 1671–1991* (St. Thomas: University of the Virgin Islands, 1992).

18. As of a July 1998 estimate, the population of the islands is approximately 118,000 persons. About 74 percent of the population is black West Indian of African descent, 5 percent Hispanic (residing primarily on St. Croix), 13 percent both black and white from the U.S. mainland, and 8 percent other. Of the West Indian population, about 45 percent are native Virgin Islanders and 29 percent immigrants from other Caribbean islands. Of the white population, a small number, resident on St. Thomas, are native-born of French descent. Their ancestors migrated to the Virgin Islands from the French Caribbean island of St. Barts in the late nineteenth century.

19. The West Indian Local Archives are described in several Danish registers and finding aids. The most recent and up-to-date register is Erik Gøbel's *A Guide to Sources for the History of the Danish West Indies (U.S. Virgin Islands), 1671–1917* (Denmark: University Press of Southern Denmark, 2002). An earlier finding aid is Wilhelm von Rosen, "Vestindiske Lokalarkiver," in *Rigsarkivet og Hjaelpemidlerne til dets Benyttelse* ["West Indian Local Archives," in *The Royal Archives and the Tools to Use Them*] (Copenhagen: National Archives, 1983).

20. Robin Sabino, in her dissertation, "Towards a Phonology of Negerhollands: An Analysis of Phonological Variation" (Ph.D. diss, University of Pennsylvania, 1990), supports the work of earlier linguists Gilbert Sprauve and Lezmore Emanual in demonstrating that the beginnings of this Creole were in Africa.

21. Dookhan, *The History of the Virgin Islands of the United States,* 193.

22. Hall, *Slave Society in the Danish West Indies,* 19.

23. This account is drawn primarily from Poul Olsen, "Negeroprør, Termitter og Landsarkiver Saxild, Om de Dansk-Vestindiske Lokalarkivers Skaebne [Negro Rebellion, Termites and the National Archivist Saxild, On the Fate of the Danish West Indies Local Archives]," trans. Pernille Levine, *Arkiv* 10 (1985): 156–75.

24. Svend E. Holsoe, "The 1848 Emancipation Rebellion on St. Croix," paper presented at the Tenth Annual Conference of Virgin Islands Historians, January 18, 1998.

25. Olsen, "Negro Rebellion,"157.

26. Because both islands had a governor, there were Government Houses, which contained the governor's residence as well as the central administrative offices in Christiansted, St. Croix, and in Charlotte Amalie, St. Thomas. Both these structures remain as working buildings today with similar functions.

27. Olsen, "Negro Rebellion," 158.

28. Olsen, "Negro Rebellion," 160.

29. Paul M. Leary, ed. *Major Political and Constitutional Documents of the United States Virgin Islands,* 107.

30. I appreciate the assistance of Poul Erik Olsen at the Danish National Archives as well as his generosity in sharing his insights on the archival implications of the treaty over several e-mail discussions.

31. Ernst Posner, "Effects of Changes of Sovereignty on Archives," *American Archivist* 5 (July 1942): 153.

32. "Annual Report of the Governor of the Virgin Islands for the Fiscal Year, 1917," unpublished manuscript, August 1, 1917, 1.

33. Rigsarkivet, Arkivvaesenets arkiv nr. 372a: Sager ang. Hjemsendelse af arkivalier fra de vestindiske oer 1896–1921. ["Report on National Archivist Saxild's Journey to the Former Danish West Indian Islands, 1919," trans. Pernille Levine.]

34. For example, in discussing his selection, Saxild mentions items he left behind, remarking, "but what use would Denmark have of records from West Indian private police cases, catalogues of personal property, auctions, regional bailiff correspondence and the like?" (7–8).

35. "Annual Report of the Governor of the Virgin Islands," unpublished manuscripts, 1917, 1918, 1919.

36. The National Archives of the United States was established in 1934. The Survey of Federal Records Project was part of the Works Project Administration, a New Deal program. The survey was sponsored by the National Archives.

37. Harold Larson, "The Danish West Indian Records in the U.S. National Archives," (St. Croix Library Association, St. Croix, Virgin Islands, 1976), photocopy; National Archives, "Accession No. 75. Records of the Danish Government of the Virgin Islands, RG 55 prepared by Harold Larson," 1937; National Archives, "Works Project Administration Central Files: State 1935–1944," RG 69, Folders 640, 660; National Archives, "Identification Inventory," Accession No. 75, 1937.

38. National Archives, "Field Service—Caribbean Area," Reports and Other Records of Field Representatives, 1942–44, RG 64, Boxes nos. 1 and 3.

39. Pamela W. Gosner, *Plantation and Town, Historic Architecture of the United States Virgin Islands* (Durham, N.C.: Moore Publishing, 1971), 103.

40. Olsen tells this story and casts doubt on it in "Negro Rebellion," 1–2.

3

RECONSTRUCTING WHOSE MEMORY? WRITING HISTORY

INTRODUCTION

"We should write the history *of* memory, observing and explaining the turbulence we find,"[1] advocates historian David Blight, who sees the historian as standing at the meeting point of the streams of memory and history. How does the history of the United States Virgin Islands promote our ability to understand its memory, and how has the removal of archival records affected the Virgin Islands's ability to write its history?

Theorists on collective memory generally agree that its construction involves the ways a society or group of people recall and define the past. They suggest that society "plays a powerful role in determining which values, facts or historical events are worth being recalled, and which are not . . . in shaping how information from the past is to be recalled . . . deciding the degree of emotional intensity to be attached to memories."[2] Although collective memory is a social construct that must be defined by the entire community and is expressed in a variety of material ways, the historian also has a role to play. On the one hand, what is remembered about the past "depends on the way it is represented, which has more to do with the present power of groups to fashion its image than with the ability of historians to evoke its memory"; on the other hand, "the historian's task is . . . to describe the images in which collective memories once lived."[3]

Medievalist Daniel Woolf offers a definition of the relationship between records, memory, and the writing of history when he divides memory into three types: personal, community, and social. Personal memory is the immediate recollections of individuals, sometimes written down but most often transmitted orally; community memory is the aggregate of personal memories, "often given permanency in communal customs, rituals, written documents or texts"; social memory is national memory, "the mediated ordering of the past of an entire nation or political community . . . into some sort of chronological account, often expressed in narrative form."[4] The interrelationships and interactions among these three modes of memory also speak to and create the notion of heritage. In tracing the development of literacy, printing, and its effects on memory, Woolf finds that the greater the proliferation of print, the less the dependence on personal and community memory in the creation of social memory. After examining the transition from an oral to a literate society in medieval England, he concludes that as printing developed and society became more educated historical sensitivity moved,

away from the local and the oral toward the national and the written; from legendary and half-legendary tales built around spatial location and isolated episode to chronologically rigorous narratives organized according to time; from a past recalled and retold in imagination, poetry, song, and casual conversation, to one contained in printed pages and constructed primarily from documentary sources.[5]

As communities move from orality to literacy, the records produced increasingly become vital building blocks of collective memory through researching and writing history and constructing formal historical narratives. The connection between records and memory has long been apparent to archivists and sociologists as well as historians. Canadian archivist Hugh Taylor notes that "visually unremarkable, voluminous in quantity, and hidden away in boxes, archives have generally been taken for granted as the information environment of traditional heritage, a collective memory to be ransacked by experts when some element of the past is to be fixed in time and space."[6] Sociologist Benedict Anderson, describing the circumstances that create the "imagined communities" of shared societal constructs, also assigns a central role to documents. Linking memory, heritage, and identity, he argues that documents in the form of newspapers, books, maps, and census records were essential in both forming national identity and the establishment of independent nations in the late eighteenth century by creating shared experiences and ideals among persons who never met but inhabited the same document space and time. In discussing the origins of national consciousness, Anderson concludes that "the convergence of capitalism and print technology on the fatal diversity of human language created the possibility of a new form of imagined community, which in its basic morphology set the stage for the modern nation."[7] The power of the archive has been identified as both a shaping and a controlling force in nineteenth-century imperialism, when deliberate and comprehensive data gathering and storage about their vast and far-flung empire was the key to the success of British colonialism.[8] One writer posits an imperial archive defined as "a fantasy of knowledge collected and united in the service of state and Empire."[9] It is an image confirmed by looking at actual practice in the colonies themselves, where colonizers who settled in a territory brought their office practices with them and established bureaucratic colonial structures that mirrored those in their home countries. When these bureaucratic officials departed, they left many of these structures behind, but not the archival practices to support them, so that archivists decades later have been confronted with a confusion of public records with no clear indications of their relationships.[10]

In the case of the Caribbean, "the separate territories involved were seen as one group with similar problems looking at them from a desk situated in the Colonial Office." Because the administration of these separate territories all followed the same pattern, documents and records were liberally inter-changed between the islands and between colonial governors and adminis-trations. Royal commissions and other monitoring groups roved around these territories "duplicating their findings and their recommendations, most of the time, leaving behind in each of the units as they passed, valuable col-lections of documents, which in the wider view one must consider as be-longing to . . . the same Archive Groups."[11] Similarly, the concept of bureaucratic organization and control through records forms a central con-struct for archival theorist David Bearman. He draws on the direct connection between the development of bureaucratic organizations in the nineteenth century and the need for centralized authority and control as governments expanded and colonized to illustrate the development of modern office sys-tems. Through the uniform application of written procedures and regula-tions, central governments could control vast holdings.[12]

At the same time, however, the identification of print technologies with these bureaucratic languages of power[13] calls into question the place of official records—and the resulting history based on those records—as reliable indi-cators of the collective memories of postcolonial societies. Michel-Rolphe Trouillot refers specifically to the chilling effect of bureaucratic power on the histories of Caribbean colonies as he catalogs the process by which archives are selected, a process involving the "selection of producers, selection of evi-dence, selection of themes, selection of procedures—which means, at best the differential ranking and, at worst, the exclusion of some producers, some evidence, some themes, some procedures."[14] Similar points can be made about the relations between records and memory in other postcolonial so-cieties. Australian Chris Healy addresses the creation of collective memory in postcolonial Australia as developed in a variety of milieus, including museums, monuments, and commemorations. He notes that in Australia, the "belief in social memory as both an elite product and an elite subject of contemplation produced much of the historical imagination of the nineteenth century to which we now have access."[15] From the Australian experience, he suggests three associations between records and social memory: the monuments that the great men of Australia left behind were in the form of paper—maps, legal documents, records, journals, and letters. Documents (rather than objects) were imagined as central to Australia's history because of its newness so that, "written or printed evidence, records, correspondence, documents, registers and census data were constituted as the key remains of history in Australia"; there was an absence of other history because Australians could find no way of representing the center of their social memory, the Aboriginal people.[16]

Although Healy presents the muting of voices of Aboriginal people in terms opposite to Trouillot's discussion of Haitian silences, the consequences are the same. In interpreting and celebrating the bicentennial of Captain Cook's voyage and in speculating on what the aborigines may have thought about it, Healy concludes that "in one case Aboriginal people could have provided an answer . . . answers could not be heard. These statements do not emerge from silence but from a seemingly endless babble about Aboriginal people created by European Australians: testimony not to silence but to the silencing of Aboriginal people." Healy suggests that it is the whole methodology of European-style history that is anathema and prevents discovery of the roots of Australian social memory. He writes, "this 'problem' is not that too many histories tell bad colonial tales too often (although they do), but [has] more to do with the habits of thinking about relationships between past and present that Australian history has encouraged; it is more to do with history itself."[17]

The negative power of bureaucratic records must also be taken into account when considering the paths of written history in former colonial societies, such as the U.S. Virgin Islands.[18] For that particular society, with its wholesale loss of records, the relation between records and history is a double-edged sword. On the one hand, if documentary sources are the building blocks of written history in a literate society, a society deprived of these building blocks also loses part of its ability to construct its memory. On the other hand, the archival power implicit in these record sources may deny the voices of the orally-based colonized people themselves. As a further example, considerations of archival power clearly come into play when assessing the written records of Native Americans. These early records, created for the most part by federal officials in the Bureau of Indian Affairs and stored in federal repositories, have created a situation in which "to be an Indian is having non-Indians control the documents from which other non-Indians write their version of your history." In 1978, historian William T. Hagan suggested that the historian, Native American or otherwise, attempt to "overcome the problems inherent in the provenance of his sources by trying to extract them from an Indian point of view." He concluded that "for the Native American this is more than just some intellectual game. What is at stake for the Indian is his historical identity, and all that can mean for self-image and psychological well-being."[19]

WRITING HISTORY WITHOUT SOURCES: HISTORY TEXTS IN THE U.S. VIRGIN ISLANDS

Hagan's conclusion might equally have applied to the Virgin Islands, whose early record situation shares much with that of Native Americans. Regardless of how records are constructed and interpreted, however, there can be little doubt that they remain essential to writing history, to the formal construction of memory, and to the narrative a community carries forward to the future. Examining the impact that the removal of the Virgin Islands archives to Denmark and the United States has had on the production of written history texts offers an opportunity to explore that relationship. Interviews with Virgin Islands researchers and analysis of the texts themselves indicate that through the loss of its records the collective memory of the community has suffered in a variety of ways, and paramount among these is the writing of history. Scholars, educators, and students alike have been equally stymied—first by distance and then by language—in attempting to access primary sources. Although the barrier of language has been largely overcome either by translation or by acquiring the necessary language skills, the logistics of distance have proved insurmountable for many (particularly in the early part of the twentieth century, when the depressed and struggling Virgin Islands community lacked both means and resources).[20] Not only is the expense of travel often prohibitive, but, as scholars have pointed out, costs of copying large amounts of material can be very high. The lack of detailed finding aids to the records has often ruled out any alternative to actually traveling to the archives.

As a consequence, research in primary sources has tended to be limited, with the few works that have used these sources becoming themselves "primary sources." The implications of these limitations have not been lost on the contemporary Virgin Islands community. As a resident of St. Croix points out, without access, "the gloss you see in a lot of the historical things that you read is simply because everybody is using the same sources." Nowhere is this more evident than in an analysis of the history texts themselves, as well as in doctoral dissertations written about Virgin Islands history. Furthermore, it is also clear that the "archival power" of the colonial record-creating administration has forced Virgin Islanders to consider alternate sources of history.

A historian at the University of the Virgin Islands laments the necessity of assigning a text of questionable scholarship because of the very few that are available. "We warn the students," she says, "and the students themselves end up realizing that it has a great number of errors and that it is slanted, but it shows you the dilemma that we have in Virgin Islands history." At the same time, an educator on St. Croix points out that "so much of our history is [by] outsiders who are looking at us, who are looking at the society, who have their biases of [their] time."[21]

Unreliable scholarship and outside interpretation characterize much of the Virgin Islands's written history. The logistical difficulties that Virgin Islanders encounter in accessing sources goes hand in hand with the problems that many small, isolated, postcolonial societies often face of being interpreted primarily by outside scholars who may have easier access to those sources. Although a corrective balance provided by histories written by scholars both within and outside the society is essential to offset the biases of both,[22] the historiographies of these small island entities also suffer from their size and relative importance. Caribbeanist and sociologist Gorden K. Lewis characterizes the historians of many of the smaller islands in the Caribbean as either local amateurs or outsider scholars with specific axes to grind. He observes that

the tiniest and most truly Lilliputian societies of the Caribbean region . . . have been curiously neglected by both West Indian and metropolitan scholarship. What local work exists has usually been done by teachers or priests struggling valiantly against tremendous odds and carries, inescapably, the mark of the amateur historian or anthropologist; correspondingly, existing scholarly work by the outsider had tended to concentrate on a single aspect of the society under investigation, thus reproducing the microscopic specialization typical of most academic research.[23]

Whether amateur or professional, scholars of Virgin Islands history have been acutely aware of the problems created by the inaccessibility of records. The introduction to *The Danish West Indies Under Company Rule, 1671–1754*, the first authoritative history of the Danish West Indies, traces the steps of its youthful Danish American author, Waldemar Westergaard, in his search for material to write his doctoral dissertation about this colony, then newly purchased by the United States. Westergaard soon discovered that "not even in the Danish language was there any reliable history of the Danish West Indies. He therefore resolved to go to Denmark and soon found that the Danish historians had neglected the history of their colonial possessions."[24] Although Danish historians have produced several major (though untranslated) historical studies, in 2002 Westergaard would not have found the situation greatly improved for English-language texts. A detailed historiography (as well as a comprehensive history) of the Danish West Indies/U.S. Virgin Islands written in English and utilizing the extensive archival resources in both Danish and English still waits for an author. Westergaard's history, published in 1919, remains the only English-language history of the Danish West Indies based on primary sources. Even that history only covers in detail the period up to 1754. Although Westergaard added a supplementary chapter bringing the history forward to 1917, he briefly skims over 160 years of major historical events.

The only two English-language accounts of the Virgin Islands written in the nineteenth century were written not by Lewis's priest and teacher but by a priest and a doctor. Even at this early stage these amateurs suffered from a lack of access to archives because many of the public records of the colonial offices were in Denmark. The Reverend John Knox's 1852 *A Historical Account of St. Thomas, W.I.* is still used (though largely anecdotal and out of print) as a text for Virgin Islands history. His major sources, as attributed in the preface, include a Dane who wrote a history of St. Thomas to 1776, a German scholar who wrote an extensive and valuable narrative of the Moravian mission to the Danish West Indies up to 1760, and a diarist whose account of life in St. Thomas spans from 1793 to 1837.[25] Although it is clear from the text that Knox also had access to local records—primarily the church records of the Dutch Reformed Church in St. Thomas, of which he was pastor—he himself recognizes the inadequacy of his sources, writing almost apologetically that "the author has attempted to combine, then fill up the gaps and continue the history to the present time. He is conscious that his book is still incomplete from inability especially to examine the public records in Copenhagen, and has not, therefore, presumed to call it a history."[26]

Dr. Charles Edwin Taylor's *Leaflets from the Danish West Indies* contains no such modest disclaimer. Written in 1888, it includes both a portrait of the author and a lengthy biographical sketch. Again, internal evidence, such as census statistics, indicates that Taylor had access to local documents, and he makes occasional reference to searches in "musty records."[27] In addition, Taylor, who ran a bookshop when he first moved to St. Thomas from England, had evidently read a wide variety of accounts of the Danish West Indies. In his discussion of recent events he often refers to journal and newspaper reports, but the text is otherwise undocumented.

Taylor cheerfully acknowledges the anecdotal nature of his writing. His goal is that "each chapter partakes of the character of an essay in which life in the Danish West Indies, that of the Danish West Indian in particular, are faithfully depicted."[28] The primary value of his book for later generations lies in his chapters on the 1848 emancipation, in which he includes the verbatim (although incomplete) translation of two eyewitness accounts of the event. These translations have been widely used by historians and have become the basis for the emancipation narrative as it has been recounted in twentieth-century history texts. Although Taylor does not credit Knox, he was apparently familiar with his work. Both authors—white, amateurs, and outsiders—wrote from a perspective that generally supported the Danish administration and society and disparaged the habits and customs of the recently emancipated slave and free colored populations. Both authors, though constantly bemoaning the difficulties of writing in a temperature of over eighty degrees Fahrenheit, have written informative though personal histories typical of their eras. Their books could fit comfortably within the context of more authoritative, source-based accounts of the period, but these do not exist.

Caribbean historian Barry Higman observes that "the historiography of the post-emancipation period [in the Caribbean] has tended to focus on a number of central issues, most, if not all, of which were concerned with the transformation of the ex-slave population into a free labour force."[29] Certainly the drive toward self-determination characterizes the post-1917 histories written by Virgin Islanders and other Caribbean historians. In contrast, those by outsiders (primarily American historians) tend either to focus on the Virgin Islands as a possession seen from the viewpoint of the United States or as a tourist destination.

Post-1917 history written in English tends to rely on Westergaard, Knox, and Taylor for accounts of the Danish colonial period. Until the 1970s these histories fell generally into the two categories suggested by Lewis: sparsely documented narratives by amateur historians (primarily Virgin Islanders) and narratives by outsiders focusing on specific issues. These amateur histories, however, were also efforts to provide an alternate history to the official version, one that spoke directly to Virgin Islanders; one that, by looking at the events of history from another point of view, fashioned a memory of which Virgin Islanders could be proud and the community could embrace. Of these histories the most influential have been written by two heroic community figures: J. Antonio Jarvis and Valdemar Hill.

Jarvis, an educator, poet, playwright, and cofounder of a major local newspaper, the *Virgin Islands Daily News* (still publishing today), wrote two history books in the 1940s and 1950s. Although drawing almost exclusively on secondary sources, Jarvis's purpose was to provide a narrative of their history to which Virgin Islanders could relate. A school principal himself, his histories were intended to educate as well as to enlighten, and they include the author's often critical and prescriptive commentary on the state of contemporary Virgin Islands society. Jarvis became so controversial in the Virgin Islands that one of his books, *The Virgin Islands and Their People*,[30] was censored by a resolution of the Virgin Islands Legislative Assembly because of its validating discussion of local folk beliefs and superstitions. In his efforts to debunk colonial myths while also providing a history text for the schools (where Virgin Islands history was not taught during the 1950s), Jarvis states in his *Brief History of the Virgin Islands* that "if history is to be useful, the author must take a firm hold of his events and personalities and mold them to a given plan without fear or favor."[31] Although his *History* contains a brief list of sources, it is clear that insufficient primary documentation forced the author to often present abrupt and sketchy accounts.

Jarvis himself was well aware of the limitations of his documentation, and this was made clear during my own interview with a St. Croix historian who related an anecdote about Jarvis being given an opportunity in the 1950s to travel to Europe to research historical records. Jarvis copied and brought back a considerable amount of material with him and told his family that he realized that he had barely scratched the surface of Virgin Islands history in his writings. To the historian, this story is apocryphal, expressing a real desire for the documents of their history on the part of Virgin Islanders. As the historian remarks, "Now this is the man who is looked upon as the dean and the best of local V.I. historians, but he was working without records and he knew that, but when he encountered the records he was aware enough to realize it."[32] In spite of these disadvantages, however, Jarvis, with his local point of view, exemplifies the historian in tune with his community, one who is seen within the society as providing a template for the type of history than can be written even with the lack of resources.

Valdemar Hill, an influential Virgin Islands politician deeply committed to greater self-government in the Virgin Islands, was a prime mover and advocate in that endeavor locally and nationally during the 1930s and 1940s. He relied on secondary sources for the pre-1917 period, and he concentrated on the African heritage that the slaves brought with them and wrote history from the viewpoint of that heritage up to emancipation and beyond. As the title of his book *(Rise to Recognition: An Account of Virgin Islanders from Slavery to Self-Government)* suggests, his primary goal was to instill a sense of pride and self-worth in his fellow citizens. Hill recognized that it was the collective nature of the struggle of an ethnic group that impelled the drive toward "freedom, self-respect, identity and self-determination." His goal in writing was to describe this collective history that the community shared. He writes, "The true history of the American Virgin Islands is not enmeshed in a succession of exploitative metropolitan governments dominating the local scene, but in the bitter and heroic struggle of an uprooted but determined people from West Africa to survive on three tiny Caribbean Islands [on] which they were forced to make their home."[33]

Histories written during this period by American historians focused on specific issues in the United States's relationship with the Virgin Islands. Charles Tansill, writing on the purchase and transfer; Luther Evans, on the American administration of the Virgin Islands up to the New Deal; and de Booy and Faris writing a travelogue-type description of the newly acquired territories used English-language archival sources available in the United States. Though their books indicate a greater ease of access to primary sources in the U.S. National Archives, for the Danish period they relied on Westergaard.[34]

In 1974, on commission from the then College of the Virgin Islands, Isaac Dookhan, a Guyanese history professor at the college, published *A History of the Virgin Islands of the United States*. Again, for the Danish period through emancipation, there was a heavy reliance on Westergaard backed up by solid and supportive use of other Danish-language secondary sources and a few English-language archives. However, for the latter part of the nineteenth century, Dookhan was able to make extensive use of Danish West Indian newspapers—as English rapidly became the lingua franca of the Danish West Indies, official announcements were printed in the newspapers in both Danish and English and thus were more accessible to a non-Danish researcher.

Shortly before Dookhan's book, *St. Croix Under Seven Flags* by Florence Lewisohn, an amateur historian and resident of St. Croix, was published in

1970.[35] Characterized as containing "ample material from both original and secondary sources [but] often anecdotal rather than analytical in approach,"[36] this is a rich though uneven history of St. Croix from its discovery to the 1960s. Lewisohn uses a wide range of sources, including those from the Danish National Archives, and it is clear from her bibliography that she used the services of a translator. Immediately on publication, Dookhan and Lewisohn became and remain the standard texts for Virgin Islands history.

Although twentieth-century Danish historians have utilized the archival sources at the Danish National Archives to produce histories of the former colony, these works have not generally been translated into English.[37] By the 1980s, however, increasing scholarly interest in reexamining and reinterpreting slavery and the slave trade, the establishment of academic scholarship in the Caribbean through the history department at the University of the West Indies, and a recognition of the richness of the Danish West Indian archives contributed to the emergence of research interest in Danish West Indian history based on a Caribbean reading of the archival record. Neville Hall, a Jamaican historian at the University of the West Indies, developed an interest in the slave societies of the Danish colonies and learned Danish to use the archives. Beginning in the 1970s, he published a series of articles on a variety of aspects of slave life that offered a completely different interpretation of Danish West Indian history—one from the viewpoint of the slaves rather than the masters.[38] Hall's untimely death in 1986 left his work unfinished. Through his insightful interpretation of the archives of slavery in the Danish West Indies, he demonstrated that careful and sympathetic scrutiny of the records of the Danish colonizers could yield the stories of their former colonials.[39]

The most recent effort at a comprehensive history of the Virgin Islands in English, however, is more reminiscent of the message-oriented writings of Jarvis and Hill than of the archival-based scholarship of Hall. *The Umbilical Cord: The History of the United States Virgin Islands from Pre-Columbian Era to the Present* uses few primary sources, relying instead on an impressive bibliography of secondary works. Like Hill, the author, Harold Willocks, a lawyer on St. Croix, is committed to writing a history for Virgin Islanders that reflects their African and Caribbean roots. In his introduction he acknowledges that one of the problems of Virgin Islands history is the lack of native writers that "causes most of the material to be written by scholars unfamiliar with the culture and the people and produces a certain degree of alienation between the writer and the history."[40]

CONTESTED HISTORY

Alienation between writer and history also speaks to the lack of access to historical records. In the U.S. Virgin Islands, this alienation has inevitably led to confrontations between history and folk narrative. In contrast to historians' researched dismissal of Pastor Weems's account of George Washington and the cherry tree, for Virgin Islanders the absence of primary sources makes it more difficult to arrive at the historical facts. An example of contested history is the legend of Buddhoe, the African hero of the successful and bloodless Emancipation Rebellion of July 3, 1848, on St. Croix in which the slaves of the Danish West Indies demanded and were given their freedom. The story suggests how and why an alternative account of historical events based on oral tradition can develop and be embraced by a community who may then reject the written records that contradict this tradition. The anecdotal sources for the rebellion survive in Charles Edwin Taylor's two eyewitness accounts published several years after the event.[41] Both accounts form the basis for legitimating Buddhoe as the champion of the rebels.

According to these accounts, Moses Gottlieb, a slave popularly dubbed General Bourdeaux or General Buddhoe, emerged as the leader of a slave conspiracy to win freedom for the enslaved population. History texts paint various romanticized pictures of Buddhoe: he rode a white horse, patrolled the mob, and kept order side by side with a Danish officer, and as the leading planner of the rebellion, he skillfully directed the rebel forces, successfully presenting the demands of the enslaved to the militia. In at least one version, he is a secret coconspirator for freedom with the governor, Peter von Scholten, and the governor's Creole mistress, Anna Heegard.[42] Following the insurrection, the Danish military quickly reestablished control, and although the Emancipation Proclamation held, a number of the rebels were subsequently tried and executed. On Buddhoe's eventual capture by the Danish militia, he was put in a boat and exiled to Trinidad (some say at his own request, others claim he was forced). His fate is unknown. One version claims that the captain of the boat had orders to kill him as soon as they sailed out of sight of land; another suggests that he prospered and lived out his life in Trinidad.

In the Virgin Islands, the name Buddhoe is synonymous with resistance and freedom, but during the year-long celebration of the 150th Anniversary of Emancipation in 1998, public controversy erupted when a Danish American historian challenged the factual underpinnings of the Buddhoe legend. The scholar had mapped the actions on that momentous July day through the records of over fifteen hundred pages of court depositions taken from former slaves in St. Croix at the trial immediately following the emancipation.[43] These court testimonies, originally delivered orally in English, were simultaneously transcribed by the court clerk into Danish and had been part of those records deposited in the Danish National Archives in 1919. To the historian, the story they told about Buddhoe's involvement differed sharply from the one that had been handed down both in folklore and in popular history texts during the 150 years since the event.

The evidence in the court testimonies and other records suggested ambi-

guities surrounding the individual known as Buddhoe, the first beginning
with his actual name, Moses Gottlieb. No one by that name was discovered
in census records, slave lists, or other records of the time, although there were
two slaves, Robert Moses and John Gottlieb, who were both active in the
insurrection events. Buddhoe may have been a conglomerate of these two
persons or, more likely, may have been John Gottlieb. In a previous study the
same scholar[44] had reconstructed events leading up to the day of the insurrection and questioned whether Gottlieb/Buddhoe had been involved in the
planning at all, although a number of other slaves were definitely identified
as being central to its conception and organization. Worse still, reconstructing
and integrating the detailed movements of a number of individuals during
the day of the rebellion itself, through a comprehensive mapping of all the
various testimonies, cast suspicion on Buddhoe's unexplained role as sudden
pacifier and controller of the angry mob. The scholar faintly suggested the
possibility that Buddhoe might have had some sort of alliance with the other
side.

Questioning Buddhoe's motives as well as his very existence stirred mixed
and ambiguous reactions within the Virgin Islands scholarly and cultural community, ranging from outright disbelief and anger to an indifferent shrugging
of shoulders. The general consensus among Virgin Islanders, however,
seemed to be first that because they themselves had little or no access to the
court records and no anticipation of future access, they were unable to as-
certain the real truth, and, second, whatever the truth, Buddhoe's significance
was as a folk hero, a symbol of emancipation rather than as an actual person.
If he was a person of dubious character, then his flaws made him all the more
human.[45] Some of the angrier reactions, however, concluded that the problem lay with the records themselves, the individuals creating them, and those
interpreting them. A guest editorial in a Virgin Islands newspaper reflects
some of the discord that the clash of histories can create:

> At discussions concerning the 1848 insurrection, I became nauseous listening to some
> of the "experts" interpreting the insurrection and the rebels. I was disgusted to listen
> to some non-Africans inform me that Buddhoe did not exist because Danish records
> did not list Moses Gottlieb as the key leader. . . . a bad feeling came over me when I
> heard non-Africans inform me that based on colonial, particularly Danish records, my
> hero(s) did not exist.[46]

Follow-up articles on the conference highlighted the controversy over the
names and very existence of Buddhoe[47] while also pointing out that because
the archives remained inaccessible, verification was all but impossible. Without these materials at hand, the newspapers concluded, "The research behind
these excellent, and to many, new presentations on slavery and emancipation
in the Virgin Islands, remains an exercise done by an elite of highly acclaimed
scholars."[48]

HOSTAGES TO HISTORY

As the Buddhoe story demonstrates, the impact of records on a community's ability to construct and maintain its collective memory can be ambiguous, even destructive. In the search for the sources of memory, written history, the accumulated product of a community of records, becomes a primary link in the ability to define the community narrative and forge community identity. Although records can support and authenticate memory, they can also question and erode it. For postcolonial societies in particular, records may play tenuous roles that rely to a great extent on the eye of the beholder, the interpreter of the records. In the case of the Buddhoe story, for example, the same court records at the Danish National Archives used for the 1998 reinterpretation of Buddhoe had been previously analyzed by Neville Hall in 1984. Similarly using the records to map the detailed movements of the rebels, Hall drew opposite conclusions and found confirmation of the Buddhoe legend through the testimony given by four former slaves condemned to execution. Extending his interpretation to embrace a wider context for slave rebellions in the Caribbean, Hall utilized this incident and its aftermath to describe a more generalized and more tragic situation in which the single-minded focus on freedom was not sufficient to keep the slaves united following emancipation itself. Hall takes the story of Buddhoe, the trials of the slaves, and Buddhoe's deportation one step further and sees the rebels, in spite of their triumph, as "vanquished victors" in the end.[49]

Although records alone may not be sufficient to tell the tale fully, they do offer frameworks for interpretation. However, competing traditions may suggest various narratives—all equally valid in their own ways—but without access to all the evidence it is difficult for the community to authenticate, evaluate, sift, and distill a memory on which it can rely. Without the ability to interpret the records for themselves, Virgin Islanders are at the mercy of interpreters, hostages to history. Regardless of any interpretations of the historical record, however, Buddhoe as a positive role model is firmly fixed within the collective memory of Virgin Islanders. Buddhoe as a historical force is legitimated through Virgin Islands history books, a statue, and a park named in his honor, as well as through vehicles of oral tradition. In the 1980s, a reconstructed folksong about Buddhoe reentered the public arena as a central part of a sixth-grade history text on the emancipation, clearly demonstrating the power of the memory of this hero and of the essential spirit of emancipation that he embodied.

Clear de road, ah yo clear de road
Clear de road leh de slave dem pass,
We a'go fo' ah we freedome

We no want no bloodshed, not a drop of bloodshed
What we want is freedom, oh gi' we ah' we freedom.

Com leh ah'we go to town, leh we meet de Gen'ral
Gen'ral name is Buddhoe, he gon gi' we freedom.

Clear de road . . .

[Clear the road, all you clear the road
Clear the road, let the slaves pass
We are going for our freedom

We don't want any bloodshed, not a drop of bloodshed
What we want is freedom, oh give us our freedom.
Come let us go to town, let us meet the General
The General's name is Buddhoe, he's going to give us our freedom

Clear the road . . .][50]

In the relationship between history and records, legitimating memory is
one of the crucial roles that records can play. In the case of Buddhoe, this
memory and the community that supports it remain vulnerable to alternative
narratives. Without recourse to records, the community can neither counter
other interpretations nor consolidate its own; without ownership of its history, it continues to be history's victim. However, the community has other
resources in addition to written ones. In the following chapter, archives take
a secondary role as the Virgin Islands community builds its collective memory
through other means.

NOTES

1. David Blight, "Historians and 'Memory,' " *Common-Place* 2(3), 2002. Online
document available at http://common-place.dreamhost.com. Accessed December 23,
2002. Emphasis in original.

2. David Gross, *Lost Time: On Remembering and Forgetting in Late Modern Culture* (Amherst: University of Massachusetts Press, 2000), 77.

3. Patrick Hutton, *History as an Art of Memory* (Hanover: University of Vermont,
1993), 7, 8.

4. Daniel Woolf, "Memory and Historical Culture in Early Modern England,"
Journal of the Canadian Historical Association 2 (1991): 285.

5. Woolf, "Memory and Historical Culture in Early Modern England," 308.

6. Hugh A. Taylor, "The Collective Memory: Archives and Libraries as Heritage,"
Archivaria 15 (Winter 1982–83): 118.

7. Benedict Anderson, *Imagined Communities: Reflections on the Origin and
Spread of Nationalism,* rev. ed. (London: Verso, 1995), 46.

8. Thomas Richards, *The Imperial Archive: Knowledge and the Fantasy of Empire*
(London: Verso, 1993).

9. Richards, *The Imperial Archive,* 6.

10. E. C. Baker, "Problems of Locating and Storing State Archival Material in Caribbean Countries," in *Report of the Caribbean Archives Conference Held at the Uni-*

versity of the West Indies, Mona, Jamaica, September 20–27, 1965 (Jamaica: University of the West Indies, n.d.). Confronting mounds of paper during the 1960s, a Jamaican archivist remarked that "there are no specific instructions anywhere on the weeding of the main bulk of records produced in the public service during the present century" (83).

11. Enos Sewlal, "Problems of Making State Archival Material Available (for Research and Other Purposes) in the Caribbean Countries," in *Report of the Caribbean Archives Conference Held at the University of the West Indies, Mona, Jamaica, September 20–27, 1965* (Jamaica: University of the West Indies, n.d.), 109.

12. David Bearman, "Diplomatics, Weberian Bureaucracy, and the Management of Electronic Records in Europe and America," in *Electronic Evidence* (Pittsburgh, Pa.: Archives and Museum Informatics, 1994), 257.

13. Anderson, *Imagined Communities,* 45.

14. Michel-Rolph Trouillot, *Silencing the Past: Power and the Production of History* (Boston: Beacon Press, 1995), 53.

15. Chris Healy, *From the Ruins of Colonialism: History as Social Memory* (Cambridge: Cambridge University Press, 1997), 91.

16. Healy, *From the Ruins of Colonialism,* 93.

17. Healy, *From the Ruins of Colonialism,* 45–46.

18. A case could be made that currently the Virgin Islands, as an "unincorporated territory" still retains colonial status. Regardless of how much local self-government Congress permits, self-government is not intrinsic to the polity of the Virgin Islands.

19. William T. Hagan, "Archival Captive—The American Indian," *American Archivist* 41 (April 1978): 142.

20. On a visit to the Virgin Islands in 1929, President Herbert Hoover famously called it "America's poor house." It was not until the 1960s, with the development of the tourist industry, that the Virgin Islands began to prosper.

21. I am grateful to Roy Adams, Marilyn Krigger, and Lauren Larsen for sharing their insights on Virgin Islands history with me.

22. The interpretation of small colonial societies and small ethnic groups is a bone of contention in many academic fields, not just history. As examples of discussion of this in relationship to Australian history and the aboriginal peoples, see Healy, *From the Ruins of Colonialism;* for the same concern in literature, see Jeannette B. Allis, "A Case for Regional Criticism of West Indian Literature," *Caribbean Quarterly* 28 (March–June 1982): 1–11.

23. Gordon K. Lewis, *The Virgin Islands: A Caribbean Lilliput* (Evanston, Ill.: Northwestern University Press, 1972), ix.

24. Waldemar Westergaard, *The Danish West Indies Under Company Rule, 1671–1754. With a Supplementary Chapter, 1755–1917* (New York: Macmillan, 1917), xviii. Some of Westergaard's research was actually done at the Bancroft Collection at the University of California, rather than at the Danish National Archives. This collection of documents from the company period and early Danish government rule was collected for H. H. Bancroft by Alphonse Pinart at the end of the nineteenth century.

25. George Høst, *Efterretninger om Øen Sanct Thomas og dens Gouverneurer, optegnede der paa Landet fra 1769 indtil 1776* (Copenhagen: Nicolaus Møller og Søn, 1791); C. G. A. Oldendorp, *Geschichte der Mission der Evangelischen Bruder auf den Caraibischen Inseln S. Thomas, S. Croix und S. Jan* (Barby: Johann Jacob Bossart, 1777); Johan Peter Nissan, *Reminiscences of a 46 Years Residence in the Island of St. Thomas in the West Indies* (Nazareth, Pa.: Senseman, 1838).

26. John P. Knox, *A Historical Account of St. Thomas, W.I.* (New York: Charles Scribner, 1852), vii–viii.

27. Charles Edwin Taylor, *Leaflets from the Danish West Indies: Social, Political, and Commercial Condition of These Islands* (London: Wm. Dawson, 1888; rpt. Westport, Conn.: Negro Universities Press, 1970), 1.

28. Taylor, *Leaflets from the Danish West Indies,* v.

29. Barry Higman, "Small Islands, Large Questions: Post-Emancipation Historiography of the Leeward Islands," in *Small Islands, Large Questions: Society, Culture and Resistance in the Post-Emancipation Caribbean,* ed. Karen Fog Olwig (London: Frank Cass, 1995), 9.

30. J. Antonio Jarvis, *The Virgin Islands and Their People* (St. Thomas: Art Shop, 1944).

31. J. Antonio Jarvis, *Brief History of the Virgin Islands* (St. Thomas: Art Shop, 1938), 7.

32. I am grateful to historian George F. Tyson for sharing his valuable insights on Jarvis and the general state of Virgin Islands history research and writing.

33. Valdemar A. Hill, *Rise to Recognition: An Account of Virgin Islanders from Slavery to Self-Government* (St. Thomas: St. Thomas Graphics, 1971), i, 178.

34. Charles Callan Tansill, *The Purchase of the Danish West Indies* (Gloucester, Mass.: Peter Smith, 1966); Luther H. Evans, *The Virgin Islands from Naval Base to New Deal* (Ann Arbor, Mich.: J. W. Edwards, 1945); Theodore de Booy and John T. Faris, *The Virgin Islands: Our New Possessions and the British Islands* (Philadelphia: J. B. Lippincott, 1918; rpt., Westport, Conn.: Negro Universities Press, 1970).

35. Florence Lewisohn, *St. Croix Under Seven Flags* (Hollywood, Fla.: Dukane Press, 1970).

36. Arnold R. Highfield and George F. Tyson, *Slavery in the Danish West Indies: A Bibliography* (St. Croix: Virgin Islands Humanities Council, 1994), 11.

37. Examples of these histories include several major works; Kay Larsen, *Dansk Vestindien 1666–1917* (Copenhagen: C. A. Reitzel, 1928) and Johannes Brøndsted, ed., *Vore Gamle Tropekolonieren* (Copenhagen: Westerman, 1952–53), 2 volumes.

38. These articles were collected and published as *Slave Society in the Danish West Indies, St. Thomas, St. John and St. Croix* (Jamaica: University of the West Indies Press, 1992).

39. Hall's colleague Barry Higman at the University of the West Indies notes in the forward to *Slave Society in the Danish West Indies* that "Neville Hall's unique contribution is to be found in his facility for language, his thorough knowledge of the Danish archives, and his ability to place his findings in a hemispheric context while taking a Caribbean perspective."

40. Harold Willocks, *The Umbilical Cord: The History of the United States Virgin Islands from Pre-Columbian Era to the Present* (Christiansted, St. Croix: Author, 1995), xxiii.

41. Two eyewitness accounts were published after the emancipation, one by Governor Peter von Scholten's brother Stadthhauptmand Chamberlain Frederik von Scholten, who describes events as he saw them from Frederiksted, and the other by Chamberlain Irminger, captain of the *Ornen.* One was recounted and published several years after the events; the other suggests a location that does not match the events being recounted. For these reasons their accuracy has been questioned. Both accounts were translated into English in the 1870s and published in 1888 by Charles Edwin

Taylor, *Leaflets from the Danish West Indies* (1888; rpt. Westport, Conn.: Negro Universities Press, 1970), 145. Because these accounts were the only primary sources easily accessible to English-language historians, they became the basic source materials for the event and remain the documents on which most accounts of the emancipation (certainly those in Virgin Islands high school history texts) have been based.

42. This composite picture is taken from several Virgin Islands history texts, including Florence Lewisohn, *St. Croix Under Seven Flags* (Hollywood, Fla.: Dukane Press, 1970), Dookhan, *A History of the Virgin Islands of the United States,* and Jarvis, *Brief History of the Virgin Islands.* The conspiracy with von Scholten is the centerpiece of the chapter on emancipation in Willocks, *The Umbilical Cord.*

43. Svend E. Holsoe presented these findings in a paper, "The 1848 Emancipation Rebellion on St. Croix," at the Tenth Annual Conference of Virgin Islands Historians, January 18, 1998.

44. Svend E. Holsoe, "The Beginning of the 1848 Emancipation Rebellion on St. Croix," in *The Danish Presence and Legacy in the Virgin Islands,* ed. Svend E Holsoe and John H. McCollum (St. Croix: Landmarks Society, 1993), 75–84.

45. In December 1998, I conducted discussions with several historians in the Virgin Islands who were familiar with this presentation. These opinions are a composite of those expressed in response to questions specifically addressing this issue.

46. Malik Sekou, "An African History of Emancipation," *Virgin Islands Daily News,* June 29, 1998, p. 12.

47. Lynda Lohr, "Buddhoe, a Man with Many Names," *Virgin Island Daily News,* February 3, 1998.

48. Janne Jorgenson, "Archival Material Needs to Come Home," *Virgin Islands Daily News,* February 3, 1998.

49. Hall, *Slave Society in the Danish West Indies,* 216, 227.

50. Marie Richards, "Clear De Road," in *Yellow Cedars Blooming: An Anthology of Virgin Islands Poetry* (St. Thomas: Virgin Islands Humanities Council, 1998), 31. Translation by Jeannette A. Bastian.

4

A COMMUNITY CONSTRUCTS ITS MEMORY: COMMEMORATIONS

INTRODUCTION

Although the relationship between records and the formal written history of a community may be more measurable and more easily discernible than that of informal oral culture, community memory is a composite of all these expressions and, as historian John Bodnar suggests, forms part of a discussion between the people and their social and political systems. Together, Bodnar argues, the people and their representatives agree on "a system of beliefs and views . . . that involves the fundamental issues relating to the entire existence of a society: its organization, structure of power, and the very meaning of its past and present."[1] To hear and witness that discussion as the memory of a community evolves means identifying those points in the life of a community when it occurs and coheres. One such focus of memory that will lead us into the collective memory of the Virgin Islands community is the commemoration of local holidays.

In his study of the celebration of the life of Abraham Lincoln, sociologist Barry Schwartz concludes that "collective memory is a representation of the past embodied in *both* historical evidence and commemorative symbolism." Nowhere is this more evident than in the Virgin Islands, where six local holidays annually celebrate the community's shared memories of the pivotal events and heroes of their history. The emphasis on the commemoration of local holidays in the Virgin Islands exemplify Schwartz's contention that "by marking events believed to be most deserving of remembrance, commemoration becomes society's moral memory. Commemoration makes society conscious of itself as it affirms its members mutual affinity and identity."[2]

The identity of a community is wrapped around the events they choose to commemorate. A glance at the list of annual local holidays in the U.S. Virgin Islands gives some good indications of the values and concerns of Virgin Islanders.

- **Transfer Day** celebrates the 1917 purchase of the islands by the United States.
- **Emancipation Day** commemorates the emancipation of the slaves in 1848.
- **D. Hamilton Jackson Day** (formerly Liberty Day) commemorates the 1915 establishment of the first free press.
- **Hurricane Supplication Day** is a day of prayer for safety through the hurricane season.
- **Hurricane Thanksgiving Day** is a day of thanks for the end of the hurricane season.
- **Organic Act Day** marks the date in 1936 that the U.S. Congress formally organized the local government of the Virgin Islands.

To this list of official holidays should be added a semi-official one, Carnival, a month-long series of events culminating in Carnival Week and a parade that involves the entire community as participants or observers. With its roots in Africa, Carnival is central to the cultural and oral traditions of many Caribbean and Latin American countries.[3]

Commemorations by their very nature tend to be both oral and physical expressions, marked by speeches, parades, presentations, monuments, and group events. These events generate a plethora of records, such as commemorative booklets, posters, mementos, photographs, videotape, and Web sites, all of which reflect as well as document the ways people celebrate the event. But it is the oral, visual, and editorial spin-offs in television, newspaper, and Internet commentary that often provide the greatest insights into expressions of public sentiment and attitudes about the celebration itself. Understanding the collective memory of a community as well as its relationship to its history includes understanding the evolving discourse around its celebrations.

In the Virgin Islands that discourse, as well as a record of the event, is often found in newspaper accounts and editorial commentary. In a part of the world where the cost of national newspapers flown in from the mainland United States is prohibitive,[4] local newspapers bear a large burden of responsibility for local and national news. In the twentieth century, the Virgin Islands has been well served by its two major local newspapers, the *St. Croix Avis*, founded in 1860 and focusing primarily on St. Croix, and the *Virgin Islands Daily News*, founded in 1932 with comprehensive coverage of all three islands. The *Virgin Islands Daily News* has historically prided itself on its community coverage, devoting at least half the newspaper, including the editorial page, to local news events. Its founders, Virgin Islanders J. Antonio Jarvis and Ariel Melchior, established a strong advocacy tradition with the newspaper serving as a political voice for its community, a strong supporter of local events, and a source of education for readers. For these reasons, local commemorations, such as Transfer Day, Emancipation Day, and D. Hamilton Jackson Day, become opportunities for the *Daily News* to inform and educate as well as report the news. During the celebrations of these events, the newspaper often adds inserts and special editions, prints archival photographs, promotes the event, publishes feature articles from people in the community, and solicits community opinion in a "person in the street" column. In addition, the paper traditionally gives space to history-related issues. For many years during the 1970s and 1980s it carried a weekly "History Corner" section. Regular weekly guest columns in recent years have featured such topics as conservation and ecology, the history of the French people of St. Thomas, and life for enslaved Africans during colonial times.

The variety of information gathered by the *Daily News* as well as its close identification with the Virgin Islands community suggest the role of a local newspaper both as reflective and expressive of collective thinking. Examining the paper's reporting of commemorative events over half a century offers an opportunity to witness the development of community consensus around specific issues. For this reason, three local holidays are selected for analysis here, each tracking the evolution of different themes within Virgin Islands life. Transfer Day, the day marking the sale and transfer of the Virgin Islands from Denmark to the United States has always been pivotal for Virgin Islanders. Responses to the annual commemorations of this day over the past 65 years reflect one facet of the ways Virgin Islanders have confronted and reconciled their memories of Danish colonialism. Celebrations of Emancipation Day reflect another, and D. Hamilton Jackson Day, memorializing events early in the American era of Virgin Islands governance, illustrates the persistent and determined evolution of a community value system of pride and self-worth.

TRANSFER DAY

> It is hereby brought to public notice that the formal delivery of the islands to the United States of America will take place this afternoon at 4 o'clock. The ceremony will be at the saluting battery.
>
> —Government of the Danish West India Islands, St. Thomas, the 31st day of March 1917[5]

On March 31, 1917, the Danish *Dannebrog* was lowered in the Barracks Yard on St. Thomas and the U.S. Stars and Stripes was raised in the official ceremony transferring ownership of the Virgin Islands from Denmark to the United States. In his *Brief History of the Virgin Islands,* J. Antonio Jarvis draws on eyewitness accounts to describe the ceremony:

Thousands of persons gathered on the ramparts of King Christian's Fort and on the surrounding hills to witness the final act of more than 50 years effort to bring the Danish West Indies under the flag of the United States.

A guard of honor from the Danish Cruiser "Valkyyrien", with the band on its right wing, drew up in front of the marine barracks, and the American guard of honor . . . faced the Danish guard. . . . In the name of his majesty King Christian the Tenth, the Danish Acting Governor, Commodore Konow proclaimed the islands transferred to the United States of America, upon which the guard of honor presented arms, the Danish flag was lowered while the Danish band played the Danish national anthem. . . . The guards of honor then changed places . . . . Commander Pollock then announced that the islands were taken into the possession of the United States, and at seven minutes before five, the American national ensign was hoisted. . . .

And thus the Danish West Indies passed into history and the Virgin Islands of the United States were born.[6]

Transfer Day is celebrated annually in the Virgin Islands on March 31 and in the 1960s became a legal holiday. It is observed at the original site of the transfer itself and often involves a reenactment of a portion of the original ceremony, generally the lowering of the Danish flag and the raising of the American flag. Danish officials as well as the Virgin Islands governor and other local politicians participate in the ceremony. Memory, history, and political action are linked in the first Transfer Day editorial in the *Daily News* in 1933. With the actual event still fresh in the minds of many citizens, the editorial voices the optimistic hope for better times that characterized public sentiment at the time of the transfer. At the same time, it expresses a generally-held disappointment in the American administration as it acknowledges that the changes hoped for by the community sixteen years ago have not come to fruition. It reaffirms the ability of Virgin Islanders themselves to persevere in spite of these setbacks.

Transfer Day will linger in the memory of those who witnessed the impressive ceremony on that hazy afternoon in March. How some wept while others rejoiced on the embankment of Fort Christian will never be forgotten. Everything then bore the softening touch of a change.

New and difficult problems handled in a different way have changed our aims from those of the past. Time too may have dealt its blows but the development of the people and the islands go on.[7]

This editorial sets the tone of future Transfer Day memorializations. Editorials and articles between 1933 and 1997 emphasize history as heritage—Danish heritage—mingled with nostalgia but also a firm belief in the endurance and progress of the Virgin Islands community. Virgin Islanders were proud and happy to be American, but they also (outwardly at least) expressed nostalgic memories and a certain respect for Denmark. This was partially based on their perception that although the Danes were class-conscious, unlike the Americans they were not overtly race-conscious and espoused equal treatment for all their citizens, including their colonials.[8] A 1957 editorial expresses this sentiment, defining racial equity as one of the focuses of Danish heritage when it notes,

It is good to honor and respect our past; to pay tribute to our rich heritage. Here all men regardless of race, creed or color are equal before the law and in their rights and they are respected and honored on their own merits, as individuals not as representatives of a certain group or clique. This is one of our prized heritage's from the Danes and it has been confirmed under the Stars and Stripes. . . . We still cherish our heritage of the past.

At the same time, the writer warns of the dangers of succumbing to nostalgia: "It is good to honor and respect our past; to pay tribute to our rich heritage under the Danes and other nationalities whose flags have flown over these islands. But it is better to peer ahead and that is what we should and must do now that we have crossed the borderline into four decades plus of Americanism."[9]

The other focus of this history-as-heritage was cultural legacy. Foods, historic architecture, and Danish street names all became "reminders of the relation of a very active present to the past. . . . Our Danish heritage is important."[10] Although Transfer Day was not commemorated through a newspaper editorial every year, it was generally noted by the population and the government in some small ceremony. The major anniversary observances—twentieth, twenty-fifth, fortieth, forty-fifth—were commemorated with elaborate reenactments of the event and generally involved speeches by invited Danish officials and local politicians. For some of these major anniversaries, the Daily News produced special supplements that included, in addition to articles on the historical details of the transfer itself, articles celebrating Danish heritage.

By 1967, the fiftieth anniversary, the emphasis was less on the nostalgia of the early years and more a celebration of becoming American. The Daily News editorial notes that "these islands are fortunate to have had such a distinguished heritage and such an impressive Transfer to commemorate,"[11] favorably comparing the joy and equanimity of the transfer between Denmark and the United States with the less happy one between the United States and Puerto Rico following the Spanish-American War.

The seventy-fifth anniversary in 1992 was officially declared a Diamond Jubilee Celebration with a commission planning festivities on all three islands. The centerpiece was a detailed reenactment of the original ceremony. An archival photograph of the original event was used as the cover for a special Transfer Day lottery drawing. The Daily News supplement included articles on all aspects of Danish heritage, with an emphasis on the material social heritage implicit in foods, language, and building styles. The underlying thread running through these articles was one of adaptation and the forging of cultural traditions through combining social elements from two worlds.

This concept coalesces in a *Daily News* article on foods written by Arona Petersen, a local authority on Virgin Islands folklore and author of several books on herbs, cooking, and folkways. In an imaginary conversation carried on in the Virgin Islands vernacular, she and a friend reminisce about preparing traditional Danish recipes with a local flavor and a moral lesson:

Like Vienna cake, we tek way fruit jam wat come wid recipe un instead use guava, guavaberry an pineapple fillin—rum instead ar brandy since we had so much rum on han (even to wash dead) to give cake diffrunt identity, so instead ar "torte" it come Vienna . . . you remember dem lil sweetbread we use to have fo Lovefeast in Sunday skule? I tink dat wat mek dey call it Lovefeast bacarse everybody useta like to feast on dem buns . . .

I tink we done jag ower memory anuff tinken bout nice ting to eat. Doan foget on udder side ar cum gat ting wat is foget fo now: Tinken bout rich food mek us foget sum time wen we even ain had coal fo coalpot, muchless food fo pot, kerosene fo lamp, houserent squeezin til back breakin.

'Tis true wat you sayin, but look wat we larn—fortitude, enduranse, pride, value, self-respeck and respeck fo udders, a firm belief in God dat never falters. We hold to all dem ting, so tis we wat get bess ar bargain, wid arl due respeck to da Danes. Tis a good feeling.

God bless America.[12]

[Like Vienna cake [for example] we took away the fruit jam that came with the recipe and instead used guava, guavaberry and pineapple filling—rum instead of brandy since we had so much on hand (even to wash the dead) to give the cake a different identity, so instead of "torte" it became Vienna . . . you remember those little sweet breads we used to have for Lovefeast in Sunday School? I think that's why they called it Lovefeast because everybody liked to feast on those little buns..

I think we've jogged our memory enough thinking about nice things to eat. Don't forget another side that we forget now: Thinking about rich food makes us forget some times when we didn't have coal in the coal pot much less food for the pot, kerosene for the lamp and house rent squeezing until you feel your back is breaking.

It's true what you're saying, but look what we learned—fortitude, endurance, pride, value, self-respect and respect for others, a firm belief in God that never falters. We hold to all those things so it is we who got the best of the bargain, with all due respect to the Danes. It's a good feeling.

God Bless America.][13]

Petersen plays on heritage to demonstrate social values while she gently mocks nostalgia. Using food as her metaphor, she illustrates not only how Virgin Islanders took Danish traditions, converted them for local use, and made them their own but also how the ability to adapt demonstrates the resilience and will to survive of the African community. When she talks about the lack of fuel and rent money, she evokes memories that the entire community can share, and she plays on these memories to show how these hard times strengthened the Virgin Islands people. Danish heritage has both positive and negative aspects. While glorying in the rich variety of food, Petersen also chides readers for getting carried away by nostalgia and forgetting the reality of life in the Danish West Indies for Virgin Islanders. She emphasizes the values of endurance and respect that those hard times built into the community and embedded into the memory as she concludes that the Virgin Islands is better off under the American flag.

The Diamond Jubilee of the transfer gave Virgin Islanders an opportunity to reassess their relationship to Denmark within the context of their own Caribbean and African identities. The Virgin Islands delegate to Congress captures this mood and sums up the general feelings of the community when he writes:

The Diamond Jubilee celebration of Transfer Day is our opportunity to put history in perspective—the history that has been written, and the history that we write as individuals and as a community with each passing day.

Our heritage, for its moments of glory and its moments of disappointments, is ours and ours alone. Who we are and what we are today has been forged in the crucibles of times and experience, a never-ending process that has given us our uniqueness and the qualities that make the people of the Virgin Islands so very special. Transfer Day speaks to the intertwining of the histories of the people of Africa and Europe, the West Indies and America.[14]

In 1993, archives became a significant (though sub-rosa) player in the Transfer Day events. The Virgin Islands government entered into negotiations with Denmark to reclaim the portion of the St. Thomas harbor and its submerged lands that according to the 1917 treaty still belonged to Denmark through its Danish West Indian Company.[15] Litigation, supported by archival documentation acquired from the Danish National Archives, did not convince the courts that the Virgin Islands could support a legitimate claim and overturn the rights granted in the treaty. However, with enthusiastic support from the community, the Virgin Islands government decided to purchase the property from Denmark. The price was $48 million, almost three times the 1917 purchase price of the entire territory. In a replay of the 1917 ceremony, the documents transferring the property were signed on March 31 in the same place and at the same time as the original transfer. Part of the property transfer included the Danish consulate, an imposing mansion overlooking the West Indian Company docks. Following the ceremonies, the governor declared the consulate an annex of Government House, moved in with his family, and held an open house for the entire community. Through the sense of satisfaction, pride, and vindication that Virgin Islanders felt in this historic reversal, the reassessment of the relationship between the Virgin Islands community and its commemoration of Transfer Day that had begun during the Diamond Jubilee entered a new phase. The *Daily News*, in a reprise of its 1933 editorial, again recognized and captured the mood of the community, noting that "there will be no weeping of joy and sorrow today as there was 76 years ago when the Dannebrog was pulled and the Stars and Stripes hoisted. . . . In what some residents consider the completion of the transfer begun in 1917, today's ceremony takes on added importance because it represents the end of Danish dominance in the territory . . . but while today signals the end of one era in our history, it is also the beginning of another era for the people of the Virgin Islands."[16]

Following this second purchase, the eightieth anniversary of Transfer Day in 1997 promoted the idea of a shared history rather than an inherited legacy. At the ceremony, the Danish foreign minister made this significant distinction by remarking that "Our common history is important, not only to understand the present times, but more importantly to understand the future. We have a shared history, I'm convinced we also have a shared future . . . in the years to come, thousands of Danes will be back [as tourists] to enjoy our shared history." A similar view of Transfer Day was summed up by a local observer who remarked that the significance of the day is as a "restatement of the feeling of brotherhood between two countries, two places that share a historical bond."[17]

From nostalgia to heritage to a shared historical bond, the evolving collective memory of the Virgin Islands community about their relationship with their colonial past is expressed in some measure through their celebration of Transfer Day. The commemoration reflects one way of reconciling a terrible, harsh past in which a people suffered the indignities not only of being sold themselves but also, as a Virgin Islander noted, of enduring a situation in which "the soil from under them [was] sold to another people and we got bought again which I don't think has happened anywhere else in the world in this century."[18] Today cultural interchange and genealogical connections between the two locations continue. Although nostalgia and heritage still remain through Friends of Denmark Societies in St. Croix and St. Thomas (who exchange visits with their Danish counterparts), clearly the community as a whole has moved beyond this to a sense of independent and parallel existence with their former colonizers. A recent agreement between the Virgin Islands and Danish governments to make the Danish West Indian archives more accessible to Virgin Islanders indicates that Denmark itself is anxious to erase any vestiges of colonialism. The collective memory of Transfer Day now consolidates positive aspects of Virgin Islands identity that recognize a justifiable pride rooted in survival and endurance, a vision of a self-sufficient future, the rejection of the colonial past, and loyalty (even gratitude) to the United States.

Transfer Day is a focused event that is well documented in official records as well as newspaper and informal accounts, as are the thirty years of negotiations leading up to the sale and the treaty.[19] In some respects, Transfer Day is ultimately all about records and transactions—the transaction of a people from one jurisdiction to another with its ironic subtext of that initial transfer and transaction from Africa. The purchase of 1993, which brought the 1917 transaction full circle, was also in a sense about records, some of which (such as the treaty) were involved in that first sale. Although these records as records figure very little in the collective memory of the event, they underpin the event itself. Within the collective memory, Transfer Day has become a successive series of attitudes and feelings that define the Virgin Islands and their relationship with both Denmark and the United States at given moments in their history. Transfer Day is a symbol, an iconography for the evolving ways that Virgin Islanders have confronted and reconciled both their relationship with their former colonial masters and their own sense of political destiny. Although the records of the event remain the background, they are nonetheless the powerful markers and symbols for that memory.

EMANCIPATION DAY AND BEYOND

While memories of Transfer Day project a benign, even philosophical face on a history of hardship and repression, other commemorations (particularly Emancipation Day) tell a different story. The distance from the event as well as its interpretive nature also mean that archives (or the lack of them) play a more prominent role in the construction of collective memory. In July 1948, the Virgin Islands commemorated the 100th anniversary of the emancipation of the slaves. The facts of emancipation, as touched on previously, are simple and straightforward. On July 3, 1848, slaves in St. Croix gathered at Fort Frederik and demanded their freedom. The Danish governor, Peter von Scholten, issued a proclamation declaring that "all unfree in the Danish West-Indian Islands are from today emancipated." Although the revolt was "marked by considerable restraint by both slaves and whites,"[20] some of the newly freed were arrested in later rioting, and several were executed. Von Scholten resigned and was court-martialed on his return to Denmark, although his proclamation was reinforced by a royal decree and von Scholten himself was later exonerated.

By the 1948 centennial of emancipation, Virgin Islanders were still grappling to establish both their economic and political independence. This is reflected in the way the event was celebrated and reported. In the context of their contemporary economic and political situation as well as rejection of the world of slavery and all it implied, freedom was very much on the minds of the Virgin Islands Municipal Council when they jointly wrote an article in the *Daily News,* "Was This a Real Freedom?" and concluded that we must be willing to break and cast away not only the formalities of a slave order but the effects of that order . . . if despite the Proclamation of 1848 a man must live in fear in order to eat and feed his family, we have much to do to make the Proclamation really worthwhile. And if it requires a change of heart and a change of mind to bring our fellowmen a real freedom, we should do that much.[21]

Despite a three-day celebration of parades and speeches, a *Daily News* editorial notes apathy toward the event and, assigning the reason to an unwillingness to confront a terrible past, comments, "there is little genuine interest locally in this important milestone of civilization. People seem anxious to forget the horrid things with which slavery is associated and to look forward to a true emancipation in all its political phases."[22]

The 150th commemoration in 1998 was honed by several decades of growing affirmation of black identity and the African cultural inheritance of Virgin Islanders as well as by greater economic stability and political self-sufficiency. Its evocation of history and memory was dramatically different from the 1948 observation. A celebration commission planned a year-long series of events that included both cultural happenings and opportunities for historical reassessment. The *Daily News* ran a regular column that explored a wide range of issues relating to slavery. In addition, opinion pieces as well as the regular news reporting of events kept emancipation continually before the community.

Some of the events specifically relating to history included the designation of Fort Frederik in Frederiksted, St. Croix, the site of the actual emancipation, as a U.S. National Historic Landmark. Two conferences on slavery and emancipation were held, one by the Society for Virgin Islands Historians and one by the University of the Virgin Islands. The Landmark Society, a historical society in St. Croix, held an exhibit of the *Fredensborg*, a sunken slave ship discovered off the coast of Norway.

These events and the newspaper stories that reported them acknowledged that dual streams of oral tradition and documented history characterized Virgin Islands culture. A guest editorial on music, for example, discussing the sustaining and inspiring qualities that music held for the enslaved Africans and the messages that the music carried, points out that "when the African's drums played or voices sang, their very sounds and utterances were acts of defiance and rebellion, and a most urgent call for freedom. Whether it was for revolt or revelry, this music was a dissonant theme in the shameful saga of slavery." The writer goes on to say that "just because there are no historical records that have actually identified and elaborated on this issue should not suggest that it did not exist."[23]

The persistent power of the oral tradition also came to bear on the Buddhoe controversy described in chapter 3. The discrepancy between the oral and the written accounts inevitably spilled over into a rehashing of the inaccessibility of archives. "Archival Material Needs to Come Home" prominently headlines a newspaper article discussing the problems for Virgin

Islanders in not having access to their archives. The author, a Danish doctoral student, points out that "it is important to note that a selective use of history is what creates myths," and that "the surface of the issues of slavery and emancipation has merely been scratched," primarily due to the fact that "the majority of archival material from Danish colonial times is held in the National Archives, Rigsarkivet, in Denmark."[24]

The 150th emancipation commemoration was only one indication that a concern for documentation was somehow coalescing with a recognition of oral tradition, African heritage, and a need to define cultural identity. Black History Month, founded in 1926 by Carter G. Woodson as an affirmation of African American identity, is observed throughout the United States every February. It is also widely observed in the Virgin Islands, and for the past decade the *Daily News* has regularly run features throughout February primarily focusing on the outstanding achievements of black Virgin Islanders. Over and over the problems posed by inaccessible archives surfaces as articles probe the implications of the lack of records. An article in a 1994 issue on family history titled "Personal History: Danish Archives Could Be Brought to V.I.," discusses various aspects of genealogy, interviews genealogists in the Virgin Islands, and lists some of the records needed to begin the search for family history. Noting that "for some Virgin Islanders, Black history is living history," the article goes on to point out that "many of the most useful Virgin Islands records aren't here. They're in Copenhagen, part of Denmark's National Archives. Genealogical Society members and others are working to have the records returned to the territory to help set up an archives."[25]

An article from 1997 also offers help for genealogists. Oral history associations on each island that have been formed to help people with family history, make "community information about local history and culture available," and collect census and church records for their members.[26] Another article uses an archival map to locate the names of plantations on St. Croix. "Almost everyone's physical address is an estate, no matter how modest. And even though the names are a reminder of plantations times, most here are loath to drop the 'estate' or change the names."[27]

At the same time, these history discussions make powerful connections between the oral tradition and collective memory. "Never turn your back on your heritage . . . never forget your source," advises Leona Watson, a teller and singer of folktales on St. Croix. She talks about growing up on the land and learning from her elders and advises young people to do the same: "If you don't know where you coming from, then you don't know where you're going. Seek knowledge. Its [*sic*] not about color. Its [*sic*] about what people are trying to make you think you are."[28]

The same issue surfaces in oral history interviews with a group of prominent senior citizens who reminisce about growing up in the 1920s. As they share their collective memories, they, like Watson, express both an awareness of the value of the oral tradition and a similar concern about passing it on:

"You asked the question earlier about the relating to this younger generation, and you heard us speak collectively of the values of our day. The question is how can we relate to them and let them know these things. It's really a tough job."[29]

Recognizing as well as reconciling the oral and the written streams of culture and history became one of the themes of an annual Summer Institute of Virgin Islands Culture established in 1997 by two professors at the University of the Virgin Islands. They blend both oral memory and documentary history when they write, "Cultural practices in the Virgin Islands are very much rooted in and operate through the oral traditions . . . a major challenge for us has been to capture the voices of Virgin Islanders conveying and expressing our culture. . . . [At the same time] there could be no meaningful discussion of Virgin Islands culture that lacked a historical underpinning."[30]

D. HAMILTON JACKSON DAY

D. Hamilton Jackson Day, November 1, commemorates an entirely different though no less self-defining event in Virgin Islands history—the biography of a Virgin Islander, David Hamilton Jackson. Born in the late nineteenth century, Jackson embodied the strivings of Virgin Islanders to achieve self-governance and political independence. A labor unionizer, newspaper publisher, and political agitator, he became known to Virgin Islanders as the Moses of his People. November 1, 1915 was the first-issue date of the *Herald,* the first locally controlled, nongovernment newspaper in the 170 years of the then Danish West Indies. Jackson, owner and editor of the paper, declared the day Liberty Day. The holiday was officially renamed for its founder in 1981.

Jackson was born in St. Croix in 1884 only thirty-six years after the Emancipation Rebellion of 1848. The harsh economic and political climate of post-emancipation St. Croix set the stage for Jackson's tremendous impact on the labor struggles of the working man and the aspirations of the black middle class. The son of a middle-class family, he was well educated, and although initially interested in becoming a Moravian minister like his father, he turned to a teaching career instead. By the beginning of the twentieth century, the small black middle class on St. Croix increasingly identified with the unskilled laborers. Franchise restrictions kept political power in the hands of the white planters and merchants; discrimination kept native Virgin Islanders out of government jobs. The black middle class felt that the Danes in Denmark were neglecting the islands. Increasingly casting themselves as the leaders of all black islanders, "racial solidarity became the glue that bound together middle and working class islanders and defined the politics of organized labor."[31] As Jackson became more involved in the social concerns of the working classes on the island, he took stands on the issues of the day and began to speak out publicly. Articulate, educated, and passionate, he quickly became a rallying point for both the workers and members of the middle class pushing for political reforms. One of his contemporaries later described Jackson's ascendance: "As the struggle between the establishment and the common man reached an impasse, it was inevitable that a man of his stature would answer the call to leadership of a people's movement with a crusader's zeal and proved to be a force to reckon with. His enemies regarded him as a fiery militant."[32]

By 1915, agricultural workers on St. Croix earned only a maximum of twenty-five cents per day. Having no way to publicly voice their concerns because newspapers were by law controlled by the government, the laborers and their middle-class supporters banded together and raised money to send Jackson to Denmark to present the complaints of black Crucians directly to King Christian X and the Danish Parliament. Jackson left for Copenhagen in 1915. Despite attempts by St. Croix planters and government officials to discredit him by calling him a firebrand and a troublemaker, cabling messages to Denmark, and printing attacks in the local newspapers, Jackson was well received in Denmark, both by the king and Parliament and by the Danish press.

In 1779, Denmark had passed a law allowing only the publication of government-subsidized newspapers on the islands. Under this law, the government also had the right to censor the news. In Denmark, Jackson argued vigorously and convincingly for repeal of this law and won his case. In addition, a private Danish association gave him a printing press. He returned to St. Croix with both the right and the means to establish a free press. In September 1915 he was welcomed home to St. Croix by joyous crowds. But Jackson realized that although he had received promises of economic and political reforms from Denmark, the economic situation in St. Croix was rapidly deteriorating. He immediately began publication of the *Herald*, calling for the workers to organize a labor union. The newly formed St. Croix Labor Union, with Jackson as their leader, called a general strike for higher wages in 1916. Five thousand plantation workers went on strike. Because the right to strike was widely accepted in Denmark, the planters did not receive support from the colonial government and, following weeks of resistance and unsuccessful stratagems by the planters, a hastily formed Planters Association agreed to negotiate with the labor union. This victory, resulting in wage increases and other favorable concessions, inspired the coal carriers on St. Thomas (primarily women) to organize into the St. Thomas Labor Union, and they also staged a successful strike for higher wages. Jackson traveled to St. Thomas, where he spoke to large, enthusiastic crowds and called for leaders to work for reforms. For the black middle class, the success of the labor unions demonstrated the "potency of mass action under capable leadership."[33]

The strikes as well as the general neglect of the islands convinced Jackson that Denmark was not committed to resolving the problems in its colonies. He began marshaling popular support for the sale of the islands to the United

States, eventually heading a local delegation to Copenhagen to demonstrate that support to the Danish Parliament. He felt that the transfer would bring equality and greater opportunity for all the people of the Virgin Islands.

Following the sale of the islands in 1917, Congress placed the Virgin Islands under the administration of the U.S. Navy, which was given all-encompassing powers over the internal affairs of the islands. Although the president appointed the governor, it was always a naval officer selected by the Secretary of the Navy. At the time of the purchase, local Virgin Islanders thought that they would automatically become U.S. citizens. However, this was not to be the case. The State Department ruled that Virgin Islanders were to be considered nationals but not citizens. The lack of citizenship and the right to vote combined with the overt racism of the navy meant that the transfer did not resolve problems for Virgin Islanders but only created new ones. The tendency of the navy to side with the planters over labor soon created new tensions between the St. Croix Labor Union and the Planters Association. Jackson continued as leader of the union, despite personal attacks on his abilities by the navy. Trumped-up charges of mismanagement of union funds, however, forced him to resign, and in 1920 he left St. Croix and went to study law in Indiana. He remained involved with the affairs of the union, however, at one point in 1921 hurrying back to St. Croix to negotiate a strike that threatened to starve the workers out.

As the sugar economy declined, political issues of citizenship and suffrage dominated the 1920s. Jackson, now a lawyer, won a seat on the St. Croix Colonial Council and, with other like-minded activists, devoted his energies to protesting naval rule in favor of a civilian government and achieving American citizenship for all Virgin Islanders. Jackson and his ilk were branded radicals by the navy and were accused of misleading the masses and promoting socialism. Jackson used the voice of the *Herald* to attack the navy and raise black consciousness and pride. Agitation by the radicals, with Jackson as one of their leaders, successfully mobilized Virgin Islanders both within the islands and in the United States. In 1926 Virgin Islanders were granted citizenship; in 1932 Congress moved the Virgin Islands to the Department of the Interior; and in 1936 Congress passed the Organic Act, the first constitution for the territory, which granted a measure of self-government over its internal affairs. Throughout these events, Jackson was an active and vocal member of various elected governing bodies of the islands. In addition to his political career, in 1931 he became a judge in the St. Croix Police Court, where he served for ten years, and was chairman of the first school board on St. Croix for fifteen years. He died in 1946 at the age of sixty-two. In the words of a contemporary, "he was the very embodiment of the charismatic leader. He led by wisdom and example, not by patronage and fear."[34]

Until Jackson's death in 1946, Liberty Day was an unofficial holiday on St. Croix, the publishing center of the *Herald*. The annual observance at Grove Place, Frederiksted, home of the St. Croix Labor Union, celebrated the successes of the labor movement and the advances made by working people since 1916. The holiday became informally known as Bull and Bread Day in honor of the feast of roast beef and rolls distributed at the first organizing meeting of the St. Croix Labor Union and traditionally served at the annual observance. The union continued to honor Jackson as its founder and inspiration. The St. Croix Labor Union offered material comfort in addition to solidarity and encouragement. Raising money through various business enterprises, they purchased land that they mortgaged to working families. These deeds were traditionally given out on Liberty Day, further enhancing the liberating significance of the day.

In 1949, the Virgin Islands Legislative Assembly passed a bill proclaiming November 1, Liberty Day, as a territory-wide legal holiday, "in recognition of the fact that the people of the three islands were the benefactors of the reforms which accrued."[35] Although Liberty Day had now become a Virgin Islands holiday, the official observance initially continued to be a labor-oriented celebration at Grove Place. In 1954, Congress passed the Revised Organic Act for the Virgin Islands, which restructured the local legislature and increased the control of locally elected officials over the internal affairs of the islands, although the governor was still appointed by the president. In 1960, for the first time, the celebration at Grove Place was attended by the governor of the islands, although the celebration still revolved around the labor union.[36] For the first time, newspapers on both St. Croix and St. Thomas reported the celebration as news. In 1961 a newly appointed governor, a local St. Thomian, attended the ceremony at Grove Place with his second-in-command, the government secretary, a native of St. Croix, who gave the keynote speech. After praising both the labor movement and Jackson, the government secretary moved into the main portion of the speech, a presentation of the proposed economic policies of the new administration. Wrapping himself and the new administration in the mantle of Jackson's legacy, the secretary exhorted the crowd to "use the occasion of Liberty Day, today and as it comes once a year to rededicate ourselves to the task of seeing that the liberties and freedoms which he [Jackson] carved out and the sacrifices which he so nobly made in the interest of improving the lot of our native workers as well as the lot of all of us shall not have been in vain."[37] The linking of Liberty Day and Jackson with contemporary political issues had begun.

In 1968, Congress passed the Elected Governor's Act, giving the Virgin Islanders the right to elect their own governor. As Virgin Islanders took control of their political system, the Liberty Day celebration became both a training ground for aspiring political candidates and a place for incumbents to solidify their support. The proximity of Liberty Day to Election Day reinforced this political connection. To the local press the closeness of the two holidays suggested yet another way Jackson's biography could be used to support current political agendas. As the 1972 editorial in the *Virgin Islands*

Daily News observed, "there is a link between Liberty Day and Election Day in more than one way. Elections are among the most visible symbols of democracy, and a free press is also an integral part of the democratic system. Therefore, it is singularly appropriate that a day commemorating a fighter for freedom of the press falls side by side with Election Day."[38]

These twin issues—freedom of the press and political struggle—rapidly became the hallmarks of the Liberty Day celebration with Jackson as their standard-bearer. Jackson became widely known as Liberty Day became an occasion for the press to repeat his biography. In 1973, the Virgin Islands Department of Education published a booklet about Liberty Day for distribution in the schools. Its purpose was to create a teacher guide about this holiday that was well known in St. Croix but not in the other islands, "in the hope that *all* Virgin Islands children will be taught the real meaning of the day."[39]

By the 1980s, the Virgin Islands press had embraced Jackson as a fellow soldier and symbolic spokesperson embodying their continuing fight for freedom of expression. Liberty Day became an unofficial Freedom of the Press Day as editorials in both major newspapers extolled the virtues of a free press and reminded the public of its importance in a democratic society. Invoking Jackson's name, they cautioned that tampering with this liberty was a betrayal of Jackson's own struggle.[40] At the same time, the proximity of Liberty Day and Election Day ensured that the holiday would continue to be a dynamic reflection of the political climate in the Virgin Islands and that politicians would bring the issues of the day to the celebration.

In 1981 the Virgin Islands Legislature approved a bill changing the name of Liberty Day to D. Hamilton Jackson Day. They recognized Jackson's role as a union organizer and as a champion of the labor movement and the right to a free press. They particularly noted his qualities of courage and conviction, as well as his love for his birthplace. By listing these qualities at the beginning of the bill, they suggested the primacy of these personal values for Virgin Islanders in evaluating Jackson's status as a hero. Changing the name of the holiday acknowledged the power of Jackson's biography over an abstraction of his accomplishments. It recognized not only the community's need for physical heroes who embodied community values but also the potential of a public holiday for perpetuating these values and instilling community pride.

Although the 1990s saw little change in the themes of D. Hamilton Jackson Day, the political aspects intensified. While newspapers continued to editorialize about freedom of the press, this was not a major part of the debate at Grove Place. The *Daily News* observed that at the 1996 celebration, "as usual, politics was the main fare for the event, despite the free roast beef and rolls given away to the throng there."[41] The decade of the 1990s in the Virgin Islands was also marked by recovery from two devastating hurricanes, Hugo in 1989, which primarily destroyed St. Croix, and Marilyn in 1995, which targeted St. Thomas and St. John. In 1995, the *Daily News* Jackson Day editorial chastised the local government for taking the public holiday and not using it as a make-up day for public schools, which were just beginning to reopen after Hurricane Marilyn. Again, using the mantle of Jackson, they wrote, "D. Hamilton Jackson would probably have been the first to urge that this year's holiday should have been observed by keeping students in school. . . . Think about it: What better use could we have made of Liberty Day 1995 than to have our students in school learning about this important and courageous Virgin Islander?"[42] At the actual celebration, the lieutenant governor asked the community to become more self-sufficient and practice some of Jackson's philosophy in the wake of Hurricane Marilyn.

In 1999, a hotly contested gubernatorial election in the Virgin Islands was inevitably reflected in the D. Hamilton Jackson Day celebration. Following speeches by the incumbent governor, the microphone was removed and the power turned off when the opposition party arrived. The challenger, later elected governor, was able to turn this show of political power to his advantage by proclaiming, "This day is Liberty Day, and it is one of the reasons people are here, because liberty (has been) endangered in the Virgin Islands. We have to teach a lesson (today) that this Virgin Islands believes in freedom."[43] When the organizers of the celebration protested that "this is not a political forum—this is where we celebrate D. Hamilton Jackson Day," an elderly Crucian observer summed up general opinion when he remarked, "It's a day to recognize the significance of Jackson, who did a lot for the Virgin Islands, and it's a day where all politicians gather to listen to the issues because it's the last day before Election Day." In an ironic twist a year later, when the new governor came to Grove Place to speak at the annual Jackson event, public schoolteachers, who were in the midst of a bitter labor strike, attended the celebration en masse and silently turned their backs when he rose to speak. This was an eloquent reminder that the original labor struggles at the core of the commemoration had not been forgotten.[44]

Although Liberty Day began as a local holiday celebrating a specific event (the founding of a newspaper), it has come to symbolize the vision of a new type of community in the Virgin Islands. The impetus that motivated poorly paid laborers to help raise the money to send Jackson to Denmark was only the first step in a process of self-realization that led to Liberty Day and beyond. Jackson not only articulated these working-class dreams but, more important, embodied the possibility of an emerging Virgin Islands society. The success of the St. Croix Labor Union and their need for an annual rallying point perpetuated Liberty Day, but the proclaiming of Liberty Day as a legal holiday ensured its place in the collective memory. Changing the name of the holiday refocused the observance on to Jackson's life and fulfilled his promise as the embodiment of Virgin Islanders' struggles. The coincidence of Liberty Day occurring on the day before Election Day also contributed to its power. As a ready-made venue for connecting physically as well as ideologically with the grassroots public so beloved of politicians, Liberty Day inevitably became synonymous with politics.

As D. Hamilton Jackson Day, the commemoration continues to redefine itself internally but never loses its center. Without changing its essence, pieces of the Jackson story have been appropriated by various groups, such as the press, who recognized that identifying with Jackson would help popularize and protect their cause. These appropriations add to the Jackson story but do not destroy its core. The significance of D. Hamilton Jackson Day may be reflected through contemporary issues, the concerns of the present may enhance or de-emphasize certain aspects of the story, but the values initially demonstrated remain the same; Jackson's life remains a lesson to be continually renewed, relearned, and redefined by Virgin Islanders for their contemporary use. The 2000 celebration, at which teachers demonstrated against the government, showed that the day not only retained its significance but, because of its iconic status within the collective memory, could be used as a powerful tool to convey a message. The teachers rejected the governor by physically turning their backs on him, and at the same time symbolically indicated that he had betrayed Jackson's struggles.

The passage of Jackson into the collective memory of generations of Virgin Islanders was foreseen at his funeral in 1946. The eulogizer observed that "we are so full of happiness today over the fact that David Hamilton Jackson lived, that we cannot indulge in grief. We, and the generations to follow us may not remember the day on which he died, but we will always remember the years in which he lived."[45]

SAILING AWAY WITH HISTORY

Commemorations in the Virgin Islands reflect a society in which oral traditions, cultural heritage, and societal values play major roles in defining the community's understanding of its history the shaping of its memory. The emphasis on and identification of heritage with history demonstrates an optimistic and determined desire to salvage and forge a positive legacy from a past overshadowed by slavery. At the beginning of the twenty-first century, that legacy has moved away from Denmark toward identification with the oral traditions and legends of the folk, the former Africans who became Virgin Islanders. Equally it has moved from a nostalgic memory of colonialism to an equal partnership with the former colonizer and participation in a shared history. At the same time, Virgin Islanders are developing their role models based on the courage, pride, and passionate commitment shown by their own local heroes.

Written records are not central to these celebrations, but at the same time, they provide a basic understanding of the historical events that undergird them. The records recounting Jackson's heroic struggles with the American government through the 1920s are all located at the National Archives in Washington. Though more accessible both by language and location than those in Denmark, they are still not easily available to Virgin Islands schoolteachers or ordinary citizens wishing to go beyond secondary sources and probe further into the primary accounts of this local hero. Because even these English-language documents are not part of the local environment, the perception running through the community of the loss of its historical records persists. It could also be argued that the ambiguity inherent in the political status of the Virgin Islands as an unincorporated territory speaks to an even more urgent need for access to the primary evidence of events, personages, and circumstances than might be true for a people more settled in their identity. But in spite of the fact that libraries in the Virgin Islands contain a number of individual microfilmed record series purchased from the archival institutions in both Denmark and Washington, there is a popular recognition that the Virgin Islands archives (and, by implication, the history of the Virgin Islands) are not easily accessible to Virgin Islanders.

In a 1975 interview in the *Daily News,* an eighty-nine-year-old resident of St. Croix, Lillian Debnam, sums up this perception when talking about researching her family history. She represents the entire community as she recounts the difficulties she encountered in trying to locate various genealogical records. " 'Can you imagine?' said Lillian, 'when the islands were sold to the United States, those old documents were taken to Denmark—with the consent of the United States! It is as though the Danes sailed off with our history, our past. If you want to see those old, old original records, you must travel to Denmark and search through that country's historical archives.' "[46]

NOTES

1. John Bodnar, "Public Memory in an American City: Commemoration in Cleveland," in *Commemorations: The Politics of National Identity,* ed. John R. Gillis (Princeton, N.J.: Princeton University Press, 1994), 75.

2. Barry Schwartz, *Abraham Lincoln and the Forge of National Memory* (Chicago: University of Chicago Press, 1999), 9, 10.

3. There is a substantial literature on the meaning of Carnival and its role. For Carnival specifically in the Virgin Islands, see Robert W. Nicholls, *Old-Time Masquerading in the U.S. Virgin Islands* (St. Thomas: V.I. Humanities Council, 1998).

4. In the Virgin Islands the current price of the daily *New York Times* is $3.50 and the cost of the Sunday *Times* is $12.

5. Public notice reproduced in J. Antonio Jarvis, *Brief History of the Virgin Islands* (St. Thomas: Art Shop, 1938), 117.

6. Jarvis, *Brief History,* 119.

7. "Transfer Day," *Virgin Islands Daily News,* March 30, 1933.

8. In an exploration of the attitudes of Virgin Islanders toward the purchase of the islands, Isaac Dookhan notes the growing alienation between native Virgin Islanders and Danish residents. This dissatisfaction was quickly converted to nostalgia after the sale. See his "Changing Patterns of Local Reaction to the United States Acquisition of the Virgin Islands, 1865–1917," *Caribbean Studies* 15 (1975): 50–72.

9. Editorial, *Virgin Islands Daily News,* April 2, 1957.

10. Editorial, *Virgin Islands Daily News,* March 30, 1966.

11. Editorial, *Virgin Islands Daily News,* March 28, 1967.

12. "How Time 'Dus' Fly," *Virgin Islands Daily News,* March 26, 1992, supplement, 62.

13. Translation by Calvin F. Bastian.

14. Ron de Lugo, *Virgin Islands Daily News,* March 26, 1992, supplement, 15.

15. Not to be confused with the Danish West India Company, which was dissolved in the eighteenth century. The Danish West Indian Company was formed by Danish businessmen in the early 1900s to try to boost the sagging economy of the Virgin Islands.

16. Editorial, *Virgin Islands Daily News,* March 31, 1993.

17. "Denmark, USVI in Harmony," *Virgin Islands Daily News,* April 1, 1997.

18. I am grateful to Gilbert Sprauve for our discussions of Virgin Islands memory.

19. For the details of the treaty negotiations, see Erik Overgaard Pedersen, "The Attempted Sale of the Danish West Indies to the United States of America, 1865–1870 (Treaties)" (Ph.D. diss., City University of New York, 1992), and Charles C. Tansill, *The Purchase of the Danish West Indies* (Gloucester, Mass.: Peter Smith, 1966).

20. Dookhan, *A History of the Virgin Islands of the United States,* 177.

21. "Was This a Real Freedom?" *Virgin Islands Daily News,* July 1, 1948.

22. Editorial, "A Century of Freedom," *Virgin Islands Daily News,* July 2, 1948.

23. Dimitri L. Copemann, "The Music of Emancipation," *Virgin Islands Daily News,* June 19, 1998.

24. Janne Jorgensen, "Archival Material Needs to Come Home," *Virgin Islands Daily News,* February 3, 1998.

25. "Personal History: Danish Archives Could Be Brought to V.I.," *Virgin Islands Daily News,* February 1, 1994.

26. Eunice Bedminster, "Genealogy: How You Can Get to the Root of Things," *Virgin Islands Daily News,* February 4, 1997.

27. Kay Johnson, "Vanity Tags, Plantation Style," *Virgin Islands Daily News,* February 14, 1994.

28. Christine Lett, "Never Turn Your Back on Your Heritage," *Virgin Islands Daily News,* February 4, 1997, supplement.

29. "Reflections of a Generation," *Virgin Islands Daily News,* February 4, 1997.

30. Gilbert Sprauve and Gene Emanuel, "Here's to Red, White and Blue—and Kallaloo Too," *Virgin Islands Daily News,* February 4, 1997, supplement, BH-8.

31. Gregory R. LaMotta, "The Americanization of the Virgin Islands, 1917–1946: Politics and Class Struggle During the First Thirty Years of American Rule" (Ph.D. diss., University of Maryland, 1992), 43.

32. Valdemar Hill Sr., "D. Hamilton Jackson . . . Moses of His People," *Virgin Islands Forum* 1 (Oct./Nov., 1973): 30.

33. LaMotta, "The Americanization of the Virgin Islands," 52.

34. Alton Adams, from his unpublished memoirs, quoted by interviewer Rosary E. Harper, "Rhetorical Analysis of Editorials Written by Two United States Virgin Islanders, David Hamilton Jackson and Rothschild Francis, During the Years 1915–1926, Compared to Arguments in Selected Speeches Delivered During the 1981 Offshore Conference" (Ph.D. diss, Florida State University, 1983), 59.

35. "Liberty Day—November 1," Booklet No. 4 printed under the auspices of ESEA Title III, Department of Education, Government of the Virgin Islands, 1968, 1.

36. *The St. Croix Avis,* November 2, 1960, 1.

37. "Liberty Day Brought Labor Reforms in V.I.," *Virgin Islands Daily News,* November 2, 1961, 6.

38. "A Man to Remember," editorial, *Virgin Islands Daily News,* November 4, 1972, reprinted in Ariel Melchior Sr., *Thoughts Along the Way: An Anthology of Editorials from the Virgin Islands Daily News, 1930–1978* (St. Thomas: Ariel Melchior, 1981), 485.

39. "Liberty Day—November 1," i.

40. In 1980, for example, the *St. Croix Avis* editorialized, "in reflection on Liberty Day, which was observed this past Saturday, it is unfortunate that the principals [*sic*] David Hamilton Jackson fought so admirably for have still not fully been adhered to." In 1981, the *Daily News* editorial observed that "Liberty Day celebrates freedom of the press—a freedom that has not always been observed in the Virgin Islands and that even now is threatened or non-existent in many part of the world, including our own Caribbean."

41. "Bull and Bread, Bryan and Brady," *Virgin Islands Daily News,* November 2–3, 1996, 1.

42. "Missed Opportunity," *Virgin Islands Daily News,* November 2, 1995, 15.

43. "Liberty (Has Been) Endangered in the Virgin Islands," *Virgin Islands Daily News,* November 3, 1998, 2.

44. "Teachers Turn Backs on Turnbull During Speech," *St. Thomas Source,* November 2, 2000. Available online at www.onepaper.com/stthomasvi. Accessed February 18, 2001.

45. *Virgin Islands Daily News,* June 4, 1946, 2.

46. "St. Croix: Remembrance of Things Past," *Virgin Islands Daily News,* August 1, 1975.

5

"GO BACK AND FETCH IT": OWNING HISTORY

INTRODUCTION

Sankofa is a proverb of the Akan people of West Africa expressed in the Akan language as "se wo were fi na wosan kofa a yenki." Literally translated it means "it is not taboo to go back and fetch what you forgot," or, in the shorter adaptation, "go back and fetch it." *Sankofa* teaches that people must go back to their roots to move forward and that whatever they have "lost, forgotten, forgone or been stripped of can be reclaimed, revived, preserved and perpetuated." Visually and symbolically *Sankofa* is expressed both as a mythic bird that flies forward while looking backward with an egg (symbolizing the future) in its mouth, or as a heartlike symbol.[1]

The concept of *Sankofa* was the motivation for both the title and the content of a folklife conference held in the U.S. Virgin Islands in 1991, "Go Back and Fetch It." Inspired by a Virgin Islands Folklife Festival sponsored by the Smithsonian Institution and held on the Mall in Washington, D.C., the previous year, panels and papers used many of the themes of the festival (such as crafts, folkways, and oral and musical traditions) to focus on defining the values of the past and demonstrating their relevance for the present. At the same time, presentations acknowledged the necessity of having control of the past to shape a viable future. In its emphasis on the importance of remembering, possessing, and transforming culture and tradition, the dictum "go back and fetch it" offers a particularly apt and fitting way to explore the nature of history in this Caribbean community, where oral traditions are more accessible than the written word. Above all, *Sankofa* reassures us that the past is there waiting to be discovered; our task is to reach back and bring it forward to be used in the present. The values inherent in understanding ourselves through our past speaks to the values of the collective memories that the community has garnered and carefully nurtured through the years. "Collective memory was stored in me," says a Virgin Islander talking about the influences that his grandmother and parents had on his understanding of his culture and society. Similarly, other Virgin Islanders reaffirm the importance of an oral memory handed down through family and through generations of culture-bearers, those persons in the community, such as folktale tellers and musicians, who embrace and cultivate the oral traditions and pass them on.[2]

The use of the sankofa bird as a logo by the State Black Archives Research Center and Museum at the University of Alabama suggests that *Sankofa* may refer to more than an oral tradition and may also symbolize a point of view about accessing the written past. For this archives, *Sankofa* "signifies the role that this repository plays in 'providing a dialogue between the present and the past.' "[3] How that dialogue can occur in a former colonial society, how the descendents of enslaved peoples can go back and fetch their history from an archives filled with the records of former masters offers challenges that speak to the very meaning and nature of the bonds between records and the communities that create them.

The interweaving threads of records, history, community, memory, and oral tradition in the U.S. Virgin Islands make clear that the collective memory of a community draws from many sources. Archives play a supporting though vital role, particularly in the grounding of that memory. For postcolonial communities, such as the Virgin Islands, however, archives seem to pose special problems that revolve around the contradictions inherent in the voice-lessness of the majority segment of a society. With no input into the record-creating process, how can these communities reclaim their history? How can the voices of those who were silent be recovered? How can communities that were the victims of records use those records to build reliable and positive constructs of their past? Such communities may superficially appear not to be communities of records at all but extreme examples of societies in which a small segment of the population produced records that controlled the lives of a disenfranchised majority. On the contrary, however, these communities share similarities with many of the silent segments of larger, more metropolitan societies who, through class, caste, or some other artificial division, seem voiceless and largely unknown but who nonetheless yearn for an identity and a history they long to find. Archives can provide the keys to that quest if the searcher recognizes that records have both a text and a subtext, that records are both evidence and action, and that behind the record lies the trace.

WITNESSES IN SPITE OF THEMSELVES

In a 1980s longitudinal sociological study of the people of St. John, Danish anthropologist Karen Fog Olwig used Danish West Indian colonial records to try to understand this post-emancipation peasant society that left no written records of its own. Olwig theorized that archival records combined with other source materials, such as oral interviews with current inhabitants of St. John who still had memories of the Danish period, could produce reliable data on the local culture. She illustrated this by using census records, land registers, and administrative reports combined with interviews to demonstrate the consolidation of land ownership and agriculture by an industrious peasantry following the 1848 emancipation. She showed that this legacy of landholding as a strong cultural value in St. John persists today. In this way, Olwig proved a viewpoint completely contrary to the previously accepted belief by Danish administrators that the people of St. John were a shiftless and unproductive peasant population.[4]

This method of historical analysis, articulated by historian Marc Bloch in the 1930s, proposes two types of historical evidence: narrative sources whose intention is to consciously inform readers, and " 'the evidence of witnesses in spite of themselves,' sources never intended to be part of the historical record." Examples of such sources include administrative records, inscriptions, and material objects. Bloch suggests that when these sources are brought together and cross-examined they "contain implicit information about the society that produced them."[5] In this methodology, "primary sources are essentially 'results' or 'traces' or 'relics' or 'tracks' of historical activity."[6] Olwig, attempting to understand the development of the culture of St. John over its 300-year history sees this method of analysis as a way of countering existing historical narratives in which "most of the descriptions of the slaves were written by planters, colonial officials, and visitors from Europe. These accounts are distorted by a misunderstanding of and negative attitudes toward people of African descent."[7] She warns, however, that the records themselves may not contain explicit accounts of the lives of slaves or their families; the historian must know the questions to bring to the historical sources. She concludes that if the records themselves can be regarded as "unintentional witnesses of Afro-Caribbean life as it is reflected in encounters between the colonial administration existing within a plantation society, the documents can yield a great deal of evidence."[8]

This view of how traces within the Danish West Indian archives can be used as a way of accessing the total society is also shared by contemporary Virgin Islanders. In discussions about the value of the Danish West Indian colonial records to the modern Virgin Islands community,[9] Virgin Islanders identified that worth in terms of finding the voices of their forebears within the subtext of official records. Virgin Islanders wanted to see and understand their history and society through the eyes and voices of their own people. The archives offered one path to discovering those voices and constructing that view. A linguist from St. John emphasizes concern with finding the authentic voices of the people in settings that are informal, natural, and vernacular. He offers an example of finding those voices in the court testimony of a Danish police court record in which he not only follows the dialogue between the witness and the lawyer but in the responses of the witness, "can hear the ticking of an intellect making sure he doesn't get entrapped by a slick lawyer."

This educator, whose research has concentrated on reconstructing Dutch Creole as a path toward understanding his own culture, emphasizes that this type of access is the only value of the records that he is interested in. "I want to get my ears as close as possible to that whisper of a people that were oppressed and have something to say."

A historic preservationist on St. Thomas (who has been actively working with the Danish National Archives to make their records more accessible to Virgin Islanders) points out that chance remarks or observations in the colonial records often contain clues to the background and origin of the slave population. For examples he points to documentary records of conversations that may indicate an African speech retention or a description of a slave village. He cautions that the danger of translations and transcriptions is that a recorder may have left out things because he did not recognize them or think them important, and these may be exactly those things that have cultural significance. He emphasizes that although the colonial records were produced by a Danish administration, "This history is linked to us, it's our history. It would not have been created if it were not for us!" This point of view is shared by many Virgin Islanders, who, though acknowledging a legitimate Danish claim to the records, also feel that their claim is equally strong. The preservationist reflects well-established community opinion as he explains that the prevailing attitude has always been that the records are Danish alone, and somehow the needs of Virgin Islanders have not been considered. But, he affirms, Virgin Islanders need access to the records to understand their past in their own way; otherwise, he points out, "anyone could tell you anything they want."

A similar point about the ownership of history is made by another St. Thomian, a political scientist with strong pan-African interests, who notes that primary source material is vital for Virgin Islanders, who essentially only have access to secondary sources written many years after the fact, because the writing of history is so dependent on who is selecting, reading, and interpreting the records. He feels that the written history on the Virgin Islands is "too planter-focused and less plantation-worker focused. It depends on whose reading the records and the records selected. How will we know!"[10]

From the viewpoint of Virgin Islanders, the administrative records of the colonizers contain at least two potential paths to the silent history of the colonized. The first occurs within the nature of the records and the record-keeping systems themselves and the information they impart through both their administrative functions and their content.[11] The second, more unconscious and accidental, relies on discovering the words or actions of the colonized, the "whispers" within the records either through transcriptions of proceedings or testimony or through observations by the record creator. Although this latter path is necessarily mediated by a third party, it can yield valuable clues to those who can recognize them.

The effect of using administrative records as tools to reconstruct the hidden society of the Danish West Indies is well demonstrated in a 1989 essay written by historian Neville Hall, who used records to describe the life and career of a nineteenth-century St. Croix freedman, Apollo Miller. Miller first comes to Hall's attention through an 1831 registry listing of free colored adult males that includes occupations; he is intrigued by Miller's listing as restaurateur, the only such one on the list. Hall explains, "Apollo Miller was thus an unusual freedman if only by virtue of the fact that in 1831 he earned his livelihood in an area void of other freedmen but himself . . . with the exception of Apollo Miller the sale of spirituous liquor by retail was a white preserve."[12] Drawing on an informed understanding of the colonial bureaucracy and the nature and purpose of the colonial records created in the Danish West Indies in the early nineteenth century, Hall uses the few records that either reference Miller or the activities in which he was involved to trace the bare bones of the man's life. He gives flesh to these bones through well-reasoned speculation about his character and activities against the backdrop of a slave society. Miller's entrepreneurial activities, not only as a restaurateur but also as a promoter of cockfights, purveyor of ice cream, and eventually innkeeper, mark him out as unusual. According to Hall, although Miller was probably literate, aside from newspaper notices advertising various activities, he personally left no records. Through official records such as registries, property records, and ordinances, Hall weaves the recorded remnants of Miller's life into the fabric of pre-emancipation colonial society on St. Croix. In this way he gives a voice as well as a form to a segment of the colonial community that had been voiceless and invisible to later generations. At the same time he presents a view of life on St. Croix from the bottom up. Hall's choice of Miller as a subject rests not only on the fact that Miller was an unusual person and an example of determination and creativity overcoming adversity; Hall was also undoubtedly influenced by the likelihood that in the search for evidence, Miller's many activities and interactions within the society increased the possibilities that there would be records about him to discover. At the same time, by selecting Miller's name from a list, Hall implies that there may be many such stories. Through the examination of the subtext of the records Hall brings a whole population to life. Certainly this interpretive use of records reinforces the concept of a meaningful record-creating presence by the black population in developing the societal values of the Virgin Islands.

In similar fashion, recent doctoral research uses census records, tax rolls, and wills to trace the histories of two generations of six "free-colored" families living in St. Croix up to the time of emancipation. None of these families left their own personal records, but the purpose of the study "was to formulate and recreate their every day living without the advantage of autobiographies, diaries, or personal firsthand writings by the subjects being investigated."[13]

Here again, records become "witnesses" to a silent society, a community that is the subject of the records rather than their maker, but one that is no less involved in their creation. From the viewpoint of the Virgin Islands, colonial records are intertwined with the growth and development of black society. Regardless of whose hand penned the records or the original administrative purpose for which they were created, the records are, in the words of one Virgin Islander, "about us."

The recognition of multiple voices within the records has also suggested ways for linguists to reconstruct as well as trace the origins of the Creole language used by the black society on St. Thomas and St. John. Researchers have found official records to be valuable sources for language study, through both the transcriptions of words and the descriptions of the origins of their subjects. The data in tax rolls and census records, for example, has suggested that African languages underpinned the development of Negerhollands (Dutch Creole) among the St. Thomas population. One such study, for example, concluded that contrary to popular notions of the enslaved,

The strength and resourcefulness of the substrate population, the demography of the St. Thomas community, and perhaps the occasional humanity of the slave-owning population enabled the speakers of Akan, Eve and Ga who were transported to the Danish West Indies in the last quarter of the 17th century, to survive long enough to begin to learn the language of their captors. In their struggle for survival as individuals and as a people, these long-forgotten men, women, and children created the language linguists have called Negerhollands.[14]

Scrutinizing Danish West Indian records through the lens of historical analysis reveals the layers of evidence that records may yield about a community. At the same time, the more layers of community that are revealed, the more blurred become many issues surrounding the record-creating process. On one hand, these are bureaucratic records created by a colonial administration operating within a colonial society; on the other hand, they reflect a completely different though parallel colonized society that exists both within and apart from the official one, a society that can be studied within the context of the records but also exists in an entirely oral way that is only hinted at in the records. Although the scholar may focus on the reconstruction of the histories and the historic traces that the records reveal, for the archivist, the overriding questions become those of context. To what extent are these records communally created as products of all segments of the society, and whose history do they reflect? What and whom are the records really about? The archival principle of provenance suggests some answers.

ARCHIVAL PROVENANCE

The principle of provenance is a fundamental concept that refers to "the organization or individual that created, accumulated, and/or maintained and used records in the conduct of business prior to their transfer to a records center."[15] This principle has undergirded archival practice since the late nineteenth century and relates to the description and maintenance of records within the environment in which they were created. Provenance is primarily concerned with identifying and safeguarding context. Though there are numerous discussions and perspectives within the archival literature about the principle of provenance and its origins,[16] archivists would generally agree first that provenance refers to the maintenance of records by their creator or source, and that second, records from different creators must not be intermingled. In the nineteenth century, archivists began to move away from the subject arrangement of archival materials toward a contextual one, an arrangement based on the idea that archival documents were not discrete items but could be best understood within the context of their creation and in relationship to other documents from the same source. Today, the principle of provenance has retained its essential core and remains the key organizational base of archival arrangement. If it has undergone any modification it has been in the direction of expanding and widening the definition of context. Provenance may be traced through individual creators, such as in a collection of personal papers, or though collective creators, as in the papers of a family. The creator may also be an entity, such as an institution or a government body, which includes many creators working within an overarching context. But the context of creation is not limited to a person or an institution. Provenance may likewise coalesce around an event or even a location.[17] As the complexity of modern records creation has put an ever-increasing burden on the principle of provenance, provenance itself has expanded to embrace both the specific processes of records production and the wider society within which the record was created. Canadian archivist Hugh Taylor noted in 1970 that "archivists ought to focus more on why and how people have created documentation, rather than on their subject content. Archivists should extend their understanding of the provenance of documentation deeply in to the societal origins of human communication throughout history."[18] Archivist Terry Cook envisions a "conceptual provenance," a provenance that "exists in the mind of the beholder." In his writings on appraisal, he suggests that in examining records and records structures, "archivists would look at the reasons for and the nature of communication between citizen and state. . . . this intellectual link to the creator thus shifts the central importance of provenance from the physical origin of the records in their creator's office to their original conceptual purpose in that same office."[19]

The principle of provenance dictates that from an archival view, the records created by the Danish government through its colonial offices rightly belong within the context of those offices and that government. This rationale—governments as the creators of the records and therefore the owners of them—gave Denmark official custody of the Danish West Indian Records and the United States custody of the Virgin Islands records created after

1917. At the same time, too narrow a construction of ownership and provenance runs the risk of not sufficiently recognizing those with equally valid
but less authoritative claims. Seen from the point of view of Cook's conceptual provenance, however, the principle of provenance envisions an archival
framework for understanding a records situation in which the native inhabitants of the Virgin Islands assume a more prominent role in both the context-
creating and the record-creating process and thus might also lay a claim to
at least co-ownership of the records.

As discussed in chapter 2, the demographics of the Danish West Indies
since its early colonization indicate the predominance of enslaved Africans.
This majority group only increased and in fact became the primary reason for
the continued existence of the colony. Following emancipation in 1848, they
formed the majority of its free citizenry. By 1917, the descendents of African
slaves, Creolized native Virgin Islanders, were the overwhelmingly majority
population of the Danish West Indies/U.S. Virgin Islands as they had been
all along. From an examination of the structure of the colonial offices as well
as the records created, clearly the enslaved African population was involved
in the record-creating process from the beginning. Whether as plantation
statistics, transactions at the auction block, objects of punishment, manu-
mitted freedmen, property transfers, testifiers in court proceedings or on police blotters, or subjects of administrative edicts or council debates, this
population was a primary subject of record-creating functions and an integral
part of the record-creating process. As free citizens, the working class and
the rising black middle class continued to be a major subject of records creation. Looking at the Danish West Indian society in retrospect, it could be
argued that from the point of view of context, the majority of the colonial
records created in the Danish West Indies concerned the non-Danish, non-
record-creating inhabitants and that the colonial society itself was the context.

Although the records were physically created by Danish clerks and other
Danish officials during the daily functioning of their offices, as in any administrative office these functions directly reflected the transactions and serviced
the needs of the whole society. In this respect, therefore, the records were
created by and within the entire colonial milieu. It could be argued, therefore,
that the colonial society within the specific locale of the Danish West Indian
islands, rather than the colonial offices in Denmark, constitute the larger
context of the records. Equally, it could also be argued that in terms of ownership, the chain of record custody does not necessarily begin with a Central
Colonial Office in Copenhagen but possibly with a small record-creating
function in St. Thomas, St. Croix, or St. John.

Extending the provenance of the creator to embrace the entire society
presents, as Cook suggests, an entirely different view of the relationships
between a community and its records, one that extends Bloch's methodology
so that the voiceless population is not the silent witness but full partner in
the record-creating process. In a community of records such as that defined

in the first chapter of this book, all layers of society are participants in the making of records, and the entire community becomes the larger provenance of the records. Seen from this view, all segments of the society have equal value.

WHO OWNS THE RECORDS?

The records created in the Virgin Islands by the Danish West Indian government and later by the American government are surrounded by the ambiguities that color all records created in colonial societies where they seem to be the joint creations of two separate populations. Who are these records about? Who actually owns these records, and who has a moral right to them? Whose history do they represent? From an archival perspective, who should have legal and physical custody of them? In 1984, the 10th International Congress on Archives suggested a solution to this dilemma by passing a resolution affirming the right of each country to the records that reflect its documentary heritage. The resolution reads in part, "the Congress reconfirms the adherence of the International Council on Archives (ICA) to its previously expressed opinion that each country should hold, within its territory, all records and archives relating to its national heritage."[20] As the Virgin Islands situation illustrates, however, this is not a simple proposition. Nor is it possible for it to be fully realized, if at all. Archival records are found in unlikely places, and many metropolitan archives contain the records of their former colonies. Although copying, microfilming, and digitization hold the promise of equal access to the dual heritage that colonizer and colonial share, logistics and cost may make these prohibitive enterprises.

The concept of joint heritage was developed by the ICA as one way of dealing with records created in colonial situations. They recognized that although the exchange of archives, primarily due to changes in sovereignty, had been customarily practiced between nations for centuries, no international procedures had ever been established. This lack of standard accepted procedures for the transfer of archives had serious consequences following the independence of colonial countries in the mid-twentieth century because "with few exceptions, the achievement of independence by the former colonies did not give rise to agreements regarding the devolution of archives."[21] Attempting to address this dilemma, the ICA defined a range of situations and conditions in which archives often became the subject of disputes and offered concrete procedures for finding resolutions. These included situations created by decolonization that could involve records created in both the colony and the metropolitan country. They acknowledged that records created during colonial administrations equally reflect the history of both the colonizer and the colonized while also producing a third historical dimension reflecting this shared relationship.[22] This recognition of dual-ownership rights or joint heritage of archival records has become an integral element in international efforts to establish procedures for the resolution of archival claims and disputes. A 1977 UNESCO report exploring the feasibility of implementing these procedures found that "with very few exceptions . . . records forming the subject of disputed claims are of interest to both parties, since they are the documentary product of a common history."[23] A corollary to this might be that a people cannot truly be masters of their own history and understand their identity unless they have access to their records.

The vital link between documentary heritage and archives is implicit in the historian's need for sources and in a larger sense in society's need for archives as the validating evidence of its own existence. A report issued in 1992 by the National Historical Publications and Records Commission, *Using the Nation's Documentary Heritage,* described documentary heritage and its relevance to each individual citizen as "the sources the nation retains so that each generation has access to its history. . . . The quality of a nation's historical understanding affects how it is governed, how citizens participate in public decisions, and the extent of community its people can achieve. Historical sources are the foundation of understanding the past." The report also points out that questions concerning these sources are of national concern and that ensuring their availability to the public "requires the combined attention of the people who use the sources, record creators and record keepers."[24]

RECORDS AND COMMUNITIES: INDIVISIBLE BONDS

Although concepts of provenance, joint custody, documentary heritage, and a need for identity affirm the strong ties between communities and the records they create, these ideas in turn find support in the many different ways in which communities define themselves. The authors of *The Presence of the Past: Popular Uses of History in American Life,* as they interviewed various ethnic groups, including African Americans, Native Americans, and Latinos, about their connections to history, noted that white Americans tended to refer to themselves and their families individually. The other ethnic groups "tended to blur the 'I' and the 'we,' " and were more likely to refer to themselves collectively, as a people.[25] Similarly, Virgin Islanders most often refer to themselves in a collective sense, as a "we" and an "us" rather than an "I." One St. Thomas educator discusses growing up in the Virgin Islands with a sense of duty to the community rather than a concern with history. "Quite frankly," he notes, "the emphasis was more on bettering yourself through education and bettering the Virgin Islands and our self-concept was based on that." He talks about the duty to educate and improve oneself so that one could in turn give back to the community. He concludes that this duty "wasn't so much a historical choice as a future imperative . . . an obligation really."

Obligation and duty to the community permeated conversations with Virgin Islanders, as did the sense of individual identity being inseparable from community identity. Although this powerful and overwhelming sense of community seemed primarily fueled by oral memories, Virgin Islanders nonetheless are fully aware of the loss of their history and perceive historical records as perhaps the only way to finally hear the voices of the colonized—within the archives of the colonizer. Pursuit of those voices is important to them as they attempt to come to terms with the legacy of slavery. As seen in the previous chapters, a corollary to this historical recognition is a growing interest in genealogy; many see this as a positive development, a path toward the historical records. Responses range widely in describing some of the most significant aspects of the Virgin Islands cultural heritage, but there is general agreement on the importance of language, resiliency and survival, family, and diversity. Both language and family speak to the importance of oral memories, not only in passing down values but also in sharing traditions. One Virgin Islander describes the oral tradition as the paramount aspect of this culture, one that not only embraces language, communication, and many features of Virgin Islands life but also binds the community together in a common identity. "It's only really understandable among Virgin Islanders," he says, and "it includes history, but it includes everything that's there, and a lot of it is history even though people don't think of it that way."[26]

Although discussions with Virgin Islanders underscored the existence of a bond between the historical record and the community, oral tradition was equally if not more significant in accessing the past. Whether a strong oral tradition persists in response to the lack of written documentation, whether the inability to possess the Danish language dispossesses Virgin Islanders from forever truly accessing their history, and whether the severe deprivation that molded this community and formed its values also affected the weight it places on written records are all questions raised rather than resolved by interviews with Virgin Islanders. These unresolved questions support indications, both within the historiography of the Virgin Islands and in the analysis of its commemorations, that having or not having access to records of necessity greatly affects the tools that are used to confront the past. It is therefore not surprising that Virgin Islanders primarily define their culture and, to some extent, their history through their oral traditions. On one hand, they do so in the absence of a written historical record, while on the other hand they follow in the footsteps of their forebears. Oral memories and oral traditions are ingrained within the heart and spirit of a people who themselves, during the 150 years of enslavement, produced few written records (or few that have survived).

At the same time, however, Virgin Islanders also recognize that they can develop a coherent understanding of their ancestors and begin to write their own history by having access to historical records. Their desire to access these records stems more from a need to know about cultural, social, and ancestral history than from any great curiosity about colonial history. They feel that the history that has been written does not reflect their voices, but they also believe that those voices exist and can be found. Virgin Islanders believe that there are moral obligations on the part of Denmark and the United States to at a minimum share this common history. Access is the all-important key; this was formally recognized by the Virgin Islands government itself in 1999 when it negotiated a bilateral agreement with the Danish Ministry of Culture for preserving and sharing historical records. Both parties to the agreement acknowledged that the removal of records to Denmark in 1917 made it difficult for Virgin Islanders to access their history and identity. At the St. Thomas ceremony for the signing of the agreement, the Danish minister noted that people "must have access to that historic information to trace families. Denmark finds it imperative to make this information available here," and the governor of the Virgin Islands agreed that documents are "historic ties to the rich and diverse cultures of both governments."[27] Both sides emphasized the importance of cooperation and respect for a common cultural heritage. They invited the National Archives of the United States to join in this endeavor to facilitate access to Virgin Islands material.[28]

The ability to access the past and to make it a vibrant part of the present is integral to the effort to go back and fetch it. Inherent in that concept is the idea that without a past that can be looked at and examined, the present cannot be fully realized. The need to be able to access the past brings us full circle in the symbiotic relationship between records, communities, and collective memory. As the case of the Virgin Islands illustrates, the community needs the records of its past to construct a reliable memory for use in the present; at the same time, written history forms only one of the ways that memory is constructed.

CONCLUSION: ACCESSING MEMORY

Few recent writings on collective memory emphasize the power of records. Perhaps this is because the influence of historical records is so pervasive that it is too obvious to mention; more likely it is due to a perception that the authentic roots of memory are to be found primarily in nonwritten public manifestations of the community, such as material culture, folkways, and celebrations. As the Virgin Islands example illustrates, however, collective memory draws from all sources in a record-creating society. The relationship between the collective memory and the society is expressed in formal ways, through the researching and writing of history, as well as through such informal means as commemoration and family history. But if the example of the Virgin Islands demonstrates that a community needs records to carry out the self-affirming activities that sustains it, it also illustrates that if records are not available, the community will replace them with something else—myth, legend, and oral tradition. A community will construct a memory regardless of the tools with which it has to work.

Though there are individual myths in any nation's psyche that persist despite proof that they have no factual base—Betsy Ross and the sewing of the first American flag, for example—this is not the same as an entire history unsupported by the availability of documentary sources that can be continually reinterpreted and reassessed. In the United States, one may look no further than current book reviews to see the constant rewriting and reconsideration of all aspects of American history by historians. Without the ability for this reassessment of its history by local historians, a community's history is vulnerable to outside interpretations, and its collective memory is fragile. There are areas, such as family history, in which research and reconstruction is impossible without records. A community without its records is a community under siege, defending itself, its identity, and its version of history without a firm foundation on which to stand.

Archivists speak of their repositories as "houses of memory," and of their records as the "corporate memory" of an institution, but in the face of so many academic diggers in the memory mines, they often seem loath to stake their claim in more definitive terms. Yet, archives as institutions—guided by the principles surrounding record creation, provenance, and custody—are unusually well equipped to support communities of records in their quest for identity. Because archivists are bound by the principles of provenance and custody, they are uniquely placed to assist in establishing the contexts of memory. With their imperative for access they are ideally placed to assist communities in retrieving their pasts, affirming the rights of communities to embrace their collective memory in all its forms, and helping communities "go back and fetch it."

NOTES

1. This definition of *Sankofa* is taken from the Web page of the Malika Kambe Umfazi Sorority at www.mku95.com/sankofa.phtml. Retrieved October 28, 2002.

2. The Folklife Festival on the Mall concentrated on demonstrating the crafts, skills, and folkways of the Virgin Islands through its culture-bearers.

3. Taken from the Web page of the Alabama University State Black Archives Research Center and Museum, http://archivemuseumcenter.mus.al.us. Retrieved October 3, 2002.

4. Karen Fog Olwig, " 'Witnesses in Spite of Themselves': Reconstructing Afro-Caribbean Culture in the Danish West Indian Archives," *Scandinavian Economic History Review* 32/2 (1984): 61–76.

5. Karen Fog Olwig, *Cultural Adaptation and Resistance on St. John* (Gainesville: University of Florida Press, 1987), 8.

6. Susan Grigg, "Archival Practice and the Foundations of Historical Method," *Journal of American History* (June 1991): 231.

7. Olwig, *Cultural Adaptation*, 8

8. Olwig, *Cultural Adaptation*, 11.

9. Between 1998 and 1999, I interviewed twenty-three persons involved in Virgin

Islands history. Seventeen lived in the Virgin Islands and eleven were Virgin Islands natives or Virgin Islanders.

10. Discussions with Virgin Islanders specifically about the value of archival records to the contemporary Virgin Islands community yielded many thoughtful and insightful responses. For their thoughts on ways of accessing history, I am particularly grateful to Gilbert A. Sprauve, Myron Jackson, and Malik Sekou.

11. From an archival standpoint, this is an example of Schellenberg's evidential value.

12. Neville A. T. Hall, "Apollo Miller, Freeman: His Life and Times," *Journal of Caribbean History* 23 (1989): 196.

13. Elizabeth Rezende, "Cultural Identity of the Free Colored in Christiansted, St. Croix, Danish West Indies 1800–1848" (Ph.D. diss., Union Institute, 1997), 4.

14. Robin Sabino, "Towards a Phonology of Negerhollands: An Analysis of Phonological Variation" (Ph.D. diss., University of Pennsylvania, 1990), 46.

15. The definition continues by stating that the principle of provenance also includes "the principle that records/archives of the same Provenance must not be intermingled with those of any other Provenance." Lewis J. Bellardo and Lynn Lady Bellardo, comps., *A Glossary for Archivists, Manuscripts Curators, and Records Managers* (Chicago: Society of American Archivists, 1992), 27.

16. See, for example, the collection of essays in *The Principle of Provenance: First Stockholm Conference on Archival Theory and the Principle of Provenance*, September 2–3, 1993 (Sweden: Swedish National Archives, 1993), and Tom Nesmith, ed., *Canadian Archival Studies and the Rediscovery of Provenance* (Metuchen, N.J.: Society of American Archivists, Association of Canadian Archivists, and Scarecrow Press, 1993).

17. In a 1980 report the Consultive Group on Canadian Archives suggesting adding to the principle of provenance, "a new corollary to the effect that any particular set of records should remain as far as possible, in the locale or milieu in which it was generated. . . . Allied to the principle of provenance is the principle of unbroken custody." Social Sciences and Humanities Research Council of Canada, Consultive Group on Canadian Archives, *Canadian Archives: Report to the Social Sciences and Humanities research Council of Canada* (Ottawa, 1980), 17.

18. Nesmith, ed., *Canadian Archival Studies and the Rediscovery of Provenance*, 17.

19. Terry Cook, "Mind over Matter: Towards a New Theory of Archival Appraisal," in *The Archival Imagination: Essays in Honour of Hugh Taylor*, ed. Barbara Craig (Ottawa, Canada: ACA, 1992), 40.

20. *Proceedings of the 10th International Congress on Archives* (Munchen: K. G. Sauer, 1986), 325.

21. Charles Kecskemeti, "Contested Records, the Legal Status of National Archives," *UNESCO Courier* (February 1985): 9.

22. Kecskemeti, "Contested Records," 9–11.

23. Charles Kecskemeti, *Archival Claims: Preliminary Study on the Principles and Criteria to be Applied in Negotiations* (Paris: UNESCO, 1977), 7.

24. Ann D.Gordon, *Using the Nation's Documentary Heritage* (Washington, D.C.: National Historical Publications and Records Commission, 1992), 13.

25. Roy Rosenzweig and David Thelen, *The Presence of the Past: Popular Uses of History in American Life* (New York: Columbia University Press, 1998), 150.

26. I appreciate the generosity of Orville Kean, Gregory LaMotta, Roy Adams, Marilyn Krigger, Derek Hodge, and Gilbert Sprauve for sharing their insights on the nature of Virgin Islands culture.

27. "Danish Archives to Be Preserved," *St. Thomas Source,* October 28, 1999. Available online at http://new.onepaper.com/stthomasvi/?v = d&i = &s = News:Local& p = 9334. Accessed November 2, 2002.

28. In 2002, the U.S. National Archives completed a detailed survey and finding aid of its Danish West Indies holdings. In October 2002, the Danish National Archives officially opened its Web site of Danish West Indian finding aids online at www. virgin-islands-history.dk/eng/default.asp.

SELECTED BIBLIOGRAPHY

Anderson, Benedict. *Imagined Communities: Reflections on the Origin and Spread of Nationalism*. Rev. ed. London: Verso, 1995.

Bearman, David. *Electronic Evidence: Strategies for Managing Records in Contemporary Organizations*. Pittsburgh, Pa.: Archives and Museum Informatics, 1994.

Bell, Wendell, and Ivar Oxaal. *Decisions of Nationhood: Political and Social Development in the British Caribbean*. Denver: Denver University Press, 1964.

Bloch, Marc. *The Historian's Craft*. New York: Vintage Books, 1953.

Booms, Hans. "Society and the Formation of a Documentary Heritage: Issues in the Appraisal of Archival Sources." *Archivaria*, 1987, 24, 69–107.

Bough, James A., and Roy C. Macridis (eds.). *Virgin Islands, America's Caribbean Outpost: The Evolution of Self-Government*. Wakefield, Mass.: Walter F. Williams, 1970.

Boyer, William W. *America's Virgin Islands: A History of Human Rights and Wrongs*. Durham,N.C.: Carolina Academic Press, 1983.

Brichford, Maynard. "The Origins of Modern European Archival Theory." *Midwestern Archivist*, 1982, 7, 87–99.

Brøndsted, Johannes (ed.). *Vore Gamle Tropekolonieren*. 2 vols. Copenhagen: Westerman, 1952–53. [Second edition, Copenhagen: Fremad, 1966–68, 8 vols.].

Caron, Aimery (comp.). *Inventory of French Documents Pertaining to the U.S. Virgin Islands, 1642–1737*. St. Thomas: Division of Libraries, Museums and Archaeological Services, 1978.

Clanchy, M. T. *From Memory to Written Record: England 1066–1307*. Oxford: Blackwell, 1993.

Connerton, Paul. *How Societies Remember*. Cambridge: Cambridge University Press, 1989.

Cook, Terry. "Electronic Records, Paper Minds: The Revolution in Information Management and Archives in the Post-Custodial and Post-Modernist Era." *Archives and Manuscripts,* 1994, *22,* 300–328.

———. "What Is Past Is Prologue: A History of Archival Ideas Since 1898, and the Future Paradigm Shift." *Archivaria,* 1997, *43,* 17–63.

Craig, Barbara (ed.). *The Archival Imagination: Essays in Honour of Hugh Taylor.* Ottawa: ACA, 1992), 40.

De Booy, Theodore, and John T. Faris. *The Virgin Islands: Our New Possessions and the British Islands.* Philadelphia: J. B. Lippincott, 1918. Reprint, Westport, Conn.: Negro Universities Press, 1970.

Dookhan, Isaac. "Changing Patterns of Local Reaction to the United States Acquisition of the Virgin Islands, 1865–1917." *Caribbean Studies,* 1975, *15,* 50–72.

———. *A History of the Virgin Islands of the United States.* Essex, England: College of the Virgin Islands, 1974.

Emanuel, Lezmore E. "Surviving Africanisms in Virgin Islands English Creole." Ph.D. diss., Howard University, 1970.

Evans, Luther H. *The Virgin Islands from Naval Base to New Deal.* Ann Arbor, Mich.: J. W. Edwards, 1945.

Falco, Nicholas. "The Empire State's Search in European Archives." *American Archivist,* 1969, *32.*

Foote, Kenneth E. *Shadowed Ground: America's Landscapes of Violence and Tragedy.* Austin: University of Texas Press, 1997.

———. "To Remember and Forget: Archives, Memory and Culture." *American Archivist,* 1990, *53,* 378–393.

Gillis, John R. (ed.). *Commemorations: The Politics of National Identity.* Princeton, N.J.: Princeton University Press, 1994.

Gøbel, Erik. "The Danish West India Company Records in the Danish National Archives." Paper presented at the annual conference of the Society of Virgin Islands Historians, St. Croix, January 16, 1988.

———. *Guide to Sources for the History of the Danish West Indies (U.S. Virgin Islands), 1671–1917.* Denmark: University Press of Southern Denmark, 2002.

Goody, Jack. *The Interface Between the Written and the Oral.* Cambridge: Cambridge University Press, 1987.

Gross, David. *Lost Time: On Remembering and Forgetting in Late Modern Culture.* Amherst: University of Massachusetts Press, 2000.

Habteyes, Lois Hassell. "Tell Me a Story About Long Time: A Study of the Folkstory Performance Tradition in the United States Virgin Islands." Ph.D. diss, University of Illinois at Urbana-Champaign, 1985.

Halbwachs, Maurice. *On Collective Memory.* Chicago: University of Chicago Press, 1992.

Hall, Neville A. T. "Apollo Miller, Freeman: His Life and Times." *Journal of Caribbean History,* 1989, *23.*

———. *Slave Society in the Danish West Indies: St. Thomas, St. John and St. Croix.* Jamaica: University of the West Indies Press, 1992.

Healy, Chris. *From the Ruins of Colonialism: History as Social Memory*. Cambridge: Cambridge University Press, 1997.

Highfield, Arnold R., and George F. Tyson. *Slavery in the Danish West Indies: A Bibliography*. St. Croix: Virgin Islands Humanities Council, 1994.

Hill, Valdemar A. *Rise to Recognition: An Account of Virgin Islanders from Slavery to Self-Government*. St. Thomas: St. Thomas Graphics, 1971.

Holsoe, Svend E., and John H. McCollum (eds.). *The Danish Presence and Legacy in the Virgin Islands*. St. Croix: Landmarks Society, 1993.

Hutton, Patrick H. *History as an Art of Memory*. Hanover: University of Vermont, 1993.

Jarvis, J. Antonio. *Brief History of the Virgin Islands*. St. Thomas: Art Shop, 1938.

————. *The Virgin Islands and Their People*. St. Thomas: Art Shop, 1944.

Jones, H. G. *Local Government Records: An Introduction to their Management, Preservation and Use*. Nashville, Tenn.: American Association for State and Local History, 1979.

Kammen, Michael G. *Mystic Chords of Memory: The Transformation of Tradition in American Culture*. New York: Vintage, 1991.

Kecskemeti, Charles. *Archival Claims: Preliminary Study on the Principles and Criteria to be Applied in Negotiations*. Paris: UNESCO, 1977.

Knox, John P. *A Historical Account of St. Thomas, W.I.* New York: Charles Scribner, 1852.

Kutzner, Jochen. "The Return of Namibian Archives." *Janus*, 1998, *2*, 34–36.

Larsen, Kay. *Dansk Vestindien 1666–1917*. Copenhagen: C. A. Reitzel, 1928.

Larson, Harold. "The Danish West Indian Records in the U.S. National Archives." St. Croix, U.S. Virgin Islands: St. Croix Library Association, 1976. Photocopy.

Leary, Paul M. (ed.). *Major Political and Constitutional Documents of the United States Virgin Islands, 1671–1991*. St. Thomas: University of the Virgin Islands, 1992.

Lewis, Gordon K. *The Virgin Islands: A Caribbean Lilliput*. Evanston, Ill.: Northwestern University Press, 1972.

Lewisohn, Florence. *St. Croix Under Seven Flags*. Hollywood, Fla.: Dukane Press, 1970.

Liebowitz, Arnold H. *Defining Status: A Comprehensive Analysis of United States Territorial Relations*. Netherlands: Kluwer, 1989.

Loftin, Joseph Evans. "The Abolition of the Danish Atlantic Slave Trade." Ph.D. diss., Louisiana State University and Agricultural Mechanical College, 1977.

Lowenthal, David. *Possessed by the Past: The Heritage Crusade and the Spoils of History*. New York: Free Press, 1996.

Maier, Pauline. *American Scripture: Making the Declaration of Independence*. New York: Vintage Books, 1997.

Martin, Henri-Jean. *The History and the Power of Writing*. Chicago: University of Chicago Press, 1994.

McBryde, Isabel (ed.). *Who Owns the Past? Papers from the Annual Symposium of the Australian Academy of the Humanities*. Melbourne: Oxford University Press, 1985.

McFerson, Hazel May. "The Impact of a Changed Racial Tradition: Race, Politics and Society in the U.S. Virgin Islands, 1917–1975." Ph.D. diss., Brandeis University, 1976.

Middleton, David, and Derek Edwards (eds.). *Collective Remembering.* London: Sage, 1997.

Muller, S., J. A. Feith, and R. Fruin. *Manual for the Arrangement and Description of Archives.* 2nd ed., trans. Arthur H. Leavitt. New York: Wilson, 1968.

Naipaul, V. S. *The Middle Passage: Impressions of Five Societies—British, French and Dutch—in the West Indies and South America.* New York: Macmillan, 1963.

Nesmith, Tom. "Seeing Archives: Postmodernism and the Changing Intellectual Place of Archives." *American Archivist,* 2002, *65,* 35.

Nesmith, Tom (ed.). *Canadian Archival Studies and the Rediscovery of Provenance.* Metuchen, N.J.: Scarecrow Press, 1993.

Nicholas, Lynn. *The Rape of Europa: The Fate of Europe's Treasures in the Third Reich and the Second World War.* New York: Vanguard, 1995.

Nissan, Johan Peter. *Reminiscences of a 46 Years' Residence in the Island of St. Thomas in the West Indies.* Nazareth, Pa.: Senseman, 1838.

Nora, Pierre. "Between Memory and History." *Representations,* 1989, *26,* 12–14.

———. *Realms of Memory,* vol.2, *The Construction of the French Past.* New York: Columbia University Press, 1992.

Olsen, Poul. "Negeropror, Termitter og Landsarkiver Saxild, Om de Dansk-Vestindiske Lokalarkivers Skaebne [Negro Rebellion, Termites and the National Archivist Saxild; On the Fate of the Danish West Indies Local Archives]." Trans. Pernille Levine. *Arkiv,* 1985, *10,* 156–175.

Olwig, Karen Fog. *Cultural Adaptation and Resistance on St. John: Three Centuries of Afro-Caribbean Life.* Gainesville: University of Florida Press, 1987.

———. " 'Witnesses in Spite of Themselves': Reconstructing Afro-Caribbean Culture in the Danish West Indian Archives." *Scandinavian Economic History Review,* 1984, *32.*

Olwig, Karen Fog (ed.). *Small Islands, Large Questions: Society, Culture and Resistance in the Post-Emancipation Caribbean.* London: Frank Cass, 1995.

Pederson, Erik Overgaard. "The Attempted Sale of the Danish West Indies to the United States of America, 1865–1870." Ph.D. Diss., City University of New York, 1992.

Posner, Ernst. *Archives in the Ancient World.* Cambridge, Mass.: Harvard University Press, 1972.

———. "Effects of Changes of Sovereignty on Archives." *American Archivist,* 1942, *5,* 141–155.

The Principle of Provenance, First Stockholm Conference on Archival Theory and the Principle of Provenance, September 2–3, 1993. Sweden: Swedish National Archives, 1993.

Rezende, Elizabeth. "Cultural Identity of the Free Colored in Christiansted, St. Croix, Danish West Indies 1800–1848." Ph.D. diss., Union Institute, 1997.

Richards, Thomas. *The Imperial Archive: Knowledge and the Fantasy of Empire.* London: Verso, 1993.

Rigsarkivet. Arkivvaesenets arkiv no. 372a: Sager ang. Hjemsendelse af arkivalier fra de vestindiske oer 1896–1921. "Report on National Archivist Saxild's Journey to the Former Danish West Indian Islands, 1919." Trans. Pernille Levine.

Rosenzweig, Roy, and David Thelen. *The Presence of the Past: Popular Uses of History in American Life.* New York: Columbia University Press, 1998.

Sabino, Robin. "Towards a Phonology of Negerhollands: An Analysis of Phonological Variation." Ph.D. diss., University of Pennsylvania, 1990.

Schellenberg, T. R. *Modern Archives: Principles and Techniques.* Chicago: University of Chicago Press, 1956.

Schwartz, Barry. *Abraham Lincoln and the Forge of National Memory.* Chicago: University of Chicago Press, 1999.

Sprauve, Gilbert A. "Chronological Implications of Discontinuity in Spoken and Written Dutch Creole." *Journal of the College of the Virgin Islands,* 1997, *5,* 40–57.

———. "Towards a Reconstruction of Virgin Islands Creole Phonology." Ph.D. diss., Princeton University, 1974.

Tansill, Charles Callan. *The Purchase of the Danish West Indies.* Gloucester, Mass.: Peter Smith, 1966.

Taylor, Charles Edwin. *Leaflets from the Danish West Indies: Social, Political, and Commercial Condition of These Islands.* London: Wm. Dawson, 1888, rpt. Westport, Conn.: Negro Universities Press, 1970.

Taylor, Hugh A. "The Collective Memory: Archives and Libraries as Heritage." *Archivaria,* 1982–83, *15,* 118–130.

———. " 'My Very Act and Deed': Some Reflections on the Role of Textual Records in the Conduct of Affairs." *American Archivist,* 1988, *51,* 456–469.

Thomas, Rosalind. *Literacy and Orality in Ancient Greece.* Cambridge: Cambridge University Press, 1992.

Trouillot, Michel-Rolph. *Silencing the Past: Power and the Production of History.* Boston: Beacon Press, 1995.

Tyson, George F. "The Historical Records of the U.S. Virgin Islands: A Report and Program Plan." Prepared for the National Endowment for the Humanities, 1977.

Tyson, George F. (ed.). *Bondsmen and Freedmen in the Danish West Indies: Scholarly Perspectives.* St. Thomas: V.I. Humanities Council, 1996).

Tyson, George F. (comp.). "Family and History Records and the U.S. and Danish National Archives." Prepared for Researching Your Roots: Genealogy in the Virgin Islands Workshop, St. Croix, May 4, 1996. Photocopy.

Upward, Frank. "Structuring the Records Continuum Part One: Post-custodial Principles and Properties." *Archives and Manuscripts,* 1996, *24,* 268–285.

van Tassel, David. *Recording America's Past, An Interpretation of the Development of Historical Studies in America, 1607–1884.* Chicago: University of Chicago Press, 1960.

Wallot, Jean-Pierre. "Building Living Memory for the History of Our Present: Perspectives on Archival Appraisal." *Journal of the Canadian Historical Association,* 1991, *2,* 282–285.

———. "Limited Identities for a Common Identity: Archivists in the Twenty-First Century." *Archivaria,* 1995, *41,* 6–30.

Westergaard, Waldemar. *The Danish West Indies Under Company Rule, 1671–1754. With a Supplementary Chapter, 1755–1917.* New York: Macmillan, 1917.

Willocks, Harold. *The Umbilical Cord: The History of the United States Virgin Islands from Pre-Columbian Era to the Present.* Christiansted, St. Croix: Author, 1995.

Wilson, Bruce G. "Bringing Home Canada's Archival Heritage: The London Office of the Public Archives of Canada, 1872–1986." *Archivaria,* 1985–86, *21.*

Woolf, Daniel. "Memory and Historical Culture in Early Modern England." *Journal of the Canadian Historical Association,* 1991, *2,* 283–308.

Index

About the Author

JEANNETTE ALLIS BASTIAN currently teaches and directs the Archives Management Program in the Graduate School of Library and Information Science at Simmons College. From 1987 to 1998 she was director of the Territorial Libraries and Archives of the United States Virgin Islands.